366 and more NATURE STORIES

by Anne-Marie Dalmais
illustrations by Annie Bonhomme
translated and edited by Colin Clark

DERRYDALE BOOKS
New York

Welcome back, swallows!

Mark hurries off towards the shed. He pushes open the heavy, wooden door which creaks on its hinges, and goes inside the huge, dimly-lit room.

He is looking for a watering-can and goes over to the corner where the tools are kept. All of a sudden, he hears a rapid beat of wings from behind him. It startles him and he turns around. "Oh, it's you, is it? You've followed me again!"

"Who? Who followed you?" asks his little sister Clare, as she enters the shed behind him.

"Why, the swallow!" Mark replies. "Every time I come here, it comes in as well. It' strange..."

"Isn't it pretty!" murmurs Clare, as she peers at the swallow.

It really is a beautiful bird: slender and streamlined, long, black wings with dark blue shades, a white chest and a dainty, long forked tail. It has a shy and trusting nature and is a fast, stylish flier, with a song that is so full of joy, it is not surprising that it is loved by everyone.

"I didn't come here to look at swallows!" exclaims Mark. "I need the watering-can; you get it, will you? I'll get the wheelbarrow. James needs it for working on the lawn down at the end of the garden."

A short while later, the two children have to go back to the shed to get some more tools for James, the gardener.

As soon as Mark and Clare go into the shed, they hear the soft rustling of the swallow's wings as it comes in after them.

"It's the same one as last time," says Mark.

"Look! It's got something in its mouth. It looks like a blade of grass," says Clare.

"Yes, I can see it too," answers Mark, a little puzzled. "I wonder what it's for... Well, it's none of our business," and he picks up the hoe and goes out, closing the door behind him.

"Mark, look!" exclaims Clare.

"Look at the strange way the swallow is flying."

In fact, the bird is flying round and round in circles in front of the door to the shed.

"Perhaps it can't stop itself," says Clare, sounding worried.

"Now I understand! I see what's going on," says Mark suddenly, dropping the hoe.

Clare looks at her brother in amazement.

"Don't you remember that last year a swallow made its nest inside the shed? It was able to get in and out whenever it wanted because there was a big hole in the door."

"But Dad repaired the hole during the Christmas holidays," continues Clare, who is beginning to understand.

"This must be the same swallow, who has come back with the spring," says Mark. "And now it can't get into the shed through the hole, so it has to wait for someone to open the door."

"Poor thing!" sighs Clare. "We have to do something to help it get in and out whenever it wants to."

No sooner said than done! The two children hurry off to find a rock to put against the door and hold it open, just enough for the swallow to get in and out.

From then on, the trusting, little swallow builds its nest a little more each day, high up under a wooden beam, in exactly the same place as the year before. For its building materials, it uses mud mixed with vegetable fibers like grass, hay and straw, which is sticks together with its own saliva. Mark and Clare follow the nest building process and notice that not only does the nest grow larger, but also more solid.

When it has finished its nest, the busy, little swallow lays its eggs in it and then broods over them for about twenty days. Then, one fine day, Clare and Mark tiptoe into the shed and hear a series of high pitched squeaks and see a line of gaping beaks around the edge of the nest.

"One, two, three, four! There are four baby swallows," whispers Mark.

"No, five!" Clare corrects him because she has spotted a fifth beak behind the others.

"Sssh... Be quiet, or you'll scare the swallow."

But the mother swallow is too busy to notice them: with all its new responsibilities, it has to spend all its time busily working to feed its five youngsters.

Daily, the little swallows are growing more and more hungry, and since they only eat insects, the parent swallow has to fly all day long around the garden, catching flies, mosquitoes, and other insects. Then it takes each tasty morsel back to one of its hungry children.

Mark and Clare watch the scene with amazement, and grow very fond of the mother swallow. She never rests, even for a moment, from the task of feeding the little birds. The two children feel proud to have played a small part in the raising of a family of five swallows. Each day, they grow more fond of the lovely swallows, and grateful to the spring which brings them.

21 Fresh, spring primroses

This morning, the sun's rays are shining more brightly than usual; they warm up the slopes of the mountains; the snow melts and the grass begins to grow.

The blackbird flies up above the rocks, higher and higher up into the sky. Then it makes a swift turn in the direction of the rock face. From there, it looks around at the meadows: "The primroses! The spring has arrived!" it seems to be saying.

The blackbird looks forward to drinking the dew drops from their petals.

22 The hare that changes color

Hop, hop, hop! Three strong leaps and the young hare comes out of its den, hidden among the roots of the fir tree.

This shy, little mountain hare is very different from its lowland cousins! Instead of being brown, it has a snowy-white coat with small patches of grey hairs; its pointed ears have black edges.

Look at it: it blends in perfectly with the surrounding countryside. In order to camouflage itself and blend into the background, this little animal changes the color of its fur according to the seasons; for this reason, one of its

names is the Varying Hare. We should try to see it during each season, so that we can check on its changes in color.

But what is it doing now? The pure white animal is racing across the snow. In order to keep itself from sinking, it spreads out its toes as far as possible. All of a sudden it stops, sniffs the warm air, and moves its little ears as it spies, not far away, little bunches of newly-opened violet crocuses!

What a surprise, after the long winter, when there is nothing else to eat but dry bark! The hare wastes no time in satisfying its hunger.

23 Protect the rare flowers!

During the warm hours of the early afternoon, Anna goes for a walk in the mountain meadows with her cousin, Mary. After walking for half an hour they reach a sunny meadow. The snow has disappeared, giving way to a carpet of little yellow, white, and violet flowers.

"Shall I pick some?" asks Anna.

"No" replies her cousin. "They must be left alone, because they can only grow here. Some of these species of flowers are in danger of becoming extinct, and may never grow again. Wouldn't that be sad?"

24 The woodchuck's winter sleep

The high mountain meadows are once again covered with flowers and look as calm and peaceful as if they were deserted. But this is only on the surface, because the woodchucks who live here are still hibernating.

In the warmth of their underground den, they are all snuggled up against each other. They have been asleep since last autumn. To make their den, they dug out a passage thirty feet long, and closed the entrance with earth and stones. In this way, the little woodchucks can sleep quietly, safe from the cold and any possible predators.

During their long, winter sleep, these little mammals remain almost completely still: they only get up five or six times. Throughout this period, the woodchucks breathe very slowly, and without realizing it they lose weight.

As soon as the spring sun warms up the air and the ground, these little animals emerge from their tunnels to feast on the fresh flowers! That is when it is easiest to see them, happily leaping around the meadows, with their sharp whistles echoing against the mountainsides.

25 The larch tree, the stream and the lark

A tall larch tree is growing beside the stream, its roots twisted around the rock.

It is a young tree and its needles, or its leaves, are very soft, growing in little bright green tufts.

The larch has spent the winter under a thick cloak of snow, while silence reigned everywhere. But now it is warmer and the snow which covered it has melted. A warm breeze caresses its long branches. Even the stream has now broken out, after long months imprisoned under a transparent crust of ice, and it is merrily swirling along.

The silver-grey water rushes over its stony bed, forming little whirlpools and spraying water up over the roots of the tree, almost as if it were bubbling along and saying: "Hooray for the spring!"

There is also a pretty lark flying from one branch of the slender larch to another, making them sway and bend. Its lively chirping is an accompaniment to the singing of the stream.

26 The noisy, neighborhood woodpecker

Tap, tap, tap! Tip, tip, tip!

"Oh no, it's starting again!" sighs the little finch.

"Will it ever stop?" complains the lively, little thrush.

"Who are they complaining about?" wonders the green woodpecker. To shut them all up it issues its harsh call, that sounds like a scornful laugh.

The woodpecker itself is a beautiful bird. It is quite large and covered with shiny feathers, yellow-green on its back and bright red on its head. With its strong beak, it hammers away endlessly on the bark of the chestnut tree. It chips out a hole with its beak, where it will make a nest.

But, on the same chestnut tree, the finch is also building its nest. This little bird has such a clear, harmonious voice that when it starts to sing everyone stops to listen to it. As for the thrush, it prefers to make its home in the cracks in walls, which it then fills with dry leaves. It is a very edgy bird with a nervous disposition. But the woodpecker does not worry about its neighbors. It just carries on until it has done what it set out to do. Tap, tap, tap!

27 Calm down, little sparrows

Clare is in her room, busy reading a book.

All of a sudden she is distracted by a noisy thumping and a deafening chorus of chirps. She runs over to the window to discover the source of all this noise. On the window ledge below, there are a dozen little birds with their feathers all puffed up. They are pushing and shoving and chasing each other. It seems as if they all want to land on the same spot.

"Calm down, little sparrows! There's room for all of you on my window ledge!"

28 Thank you, friendly blackbird

"That's the blackbird!" thinks Mark as soon as he wakes up. Unlike most other mornings, he jumps out of bed and rushes to the window. "Thank you, friendly blackbird, for coming back to our garden again this year!"

Mark hasn't even opened the heavy wooden shutters on the window, but already he has recognized the blackbird's happy song.

Now the boy can see it hopping on the freshly cut lawn. Its bright yellow beak stands out against its shiny jet black plumage. Nothing is more pleasant, after the long winter silence, than being woken up again by this cheerful song.

But, oh look... our blackbird is not alone! Beside him is a dainty female, covered in brown feathers, and holding a long blade of grass in her beak.

"I see!" exclaims Mark. "This pair is nest-building."

Mark knows that blackbirds make their nests for their young in the forked branches of trees, using grass, and mud.

"Thank you, thank you, friendly blackbirds for bringing new life to the garden again."

29 The surprise in the mailbox

Do you know what Jenny does on Saturdays, as soon as she arrives with her parents at their country house? She pushes open the gate and rushes to open the mailbox which is fastened to the fence.

She is always very curious to see how much mail has arrived during the week. But this time, she gets a big surprise. Instead of the usual letters, she finds a lovely nest containing two little birds inside.

"Mom, dad, come and see!" calls Jenny, very excited by her discovery. Her mother comes to have a look.

From the little, blue-black heads and yellow-blue feathers, she recognizes the birds immediately as graceful little blue larks.

"They must have decided to make their home in the mailbox," she says. "We mustn't disturb these little birds: we'll have to tell the mailman to put the mail on the doorstep. And if you are careful, Jenny, you'll be able to watch the birth of a new family!"

And, of course, Jenny is much happier now than she would have been, had she found a whole pile of letters in the box!

30 The thistle-hunting goldfinch

The goldfinch gets its name from the lovely, golden-yellow color of the band of feathers on its wings.

But did you know that goldfinches can often be found flying in and out of clusters of thistles. What do you think they are doing in among such prickly plants? Eating them? No! The goldfinch gathers up the furry seeds of the thistle and covers its nest with them, to make it soft and fluffy.

31 The firecrest, a little king

If we look at this tiny bird, with its delicate crown of orange feathers bordered with black and its elegant olive-green back, we can see why the firecrest is sometimes nicknamed "the little king". It is a very lively little bird which spreads its insistent, penetrating, imperious call everywhere it goes.

The firecrest builds a very special nest so skilfully that it is amazingly light. With thin strands of moss, the firecrest creates a semicircular sack, hanging it between two fir or pine twigs.

It is remarkable that the little sack of moss stays up, hanging in this way. It does so because the little bird is itself so light that its weight barely bends the branch the nest hangs from.

There is also another reason why the nest is so light. In order to support it better and keep it secured, the firecrest strengthens it with a very fine "net" of spiders' webs.

Our little firecrest is very ingenious, don't you think?

1 Where do you come from, little goldfish?

Looking into the transparent glass bowl, Matthew studies his little goldfish. It swims around and around, brushing the walls of the bowl; it swims up to the surface, then, leaving a trail of bubbles, it swims, round some more, before going down to rest by the white pebbles on the bottom, holding its position with occasional flicks of its tail.

"Where do you come from, little goldfish?" Matthew wonders. But as he touches the bowl with his finger the goldfish just gives a little wriggle.

2 The ladybug wakes up

The midday sun warms the window panes, and the room where Elizabeth is playing with her dolls begins to warm up.

The heat is very pleasant and peaceful.

A ladybug has been sleeping in the thick folds of the curtains, and suddenly wakes up. The sun, just like the prince who wakens the Sleeping Beauty, has brought it out of its long rest. Protected by the soft folds of the curtain, the ladybug has been sleeping there since autumn. It slept so deeply that it stayed completely still: it looked as if it were dead.

But it has been slowly brought back to life by the warmth. Now it moves its feet, then its antennae, and, ready for adventure, right in front of Elizabeth's eyes, this little, live, red dot, on the huge expanse of soft, warm curtain, begins to flutter its wings.

"A ladybug," cries Elizabeth, hurrying over to the window. She studies the graceful, little insect, and peers at the bright, red, hard, shell-like body, shiny and dotted with little black spots.

"Isn't it pretty!" she exclaims. "And it's a good luck sign too!"

3 The magic of springtime

As if by magic Laura's garden has suddenly filled up with flowers: it is the magic of springtime.

Just a few weeks ago the earth was flat, dark, and bare. But now, look at it! It is covered in flowers: lots of different flowers standing straight up on their stems and opening their petals to the sunlight!

There are narcissi and bright, yellow jonquils; pale blue and pink hyacinths; splendid, bright-colored tulips: red, yellow, purple: what a wonderful garland.

Do you know the secret of this wonderful sight? In the autumn, Laura had helped her mother plant the tulip bulbs, which looked like large onions. She had dug a little hole in the ground for each bulb, then she had put the bulb in the hole and covered it with earth. The bulbs slept in their holes right through the winter. With the coming of spring, they put out their tender, green shoots, then their stalks, and, finally, all of a sudden, their flowers opened up.

Laura understands that nature works these miracles. In order to grow, the bulb, which is a seed, had to be nourished by the earth, water, and the warm light of the sun.

4 The ribbon that flew away

"I can't find the green ribbon for my hair anywhere," says Jenny.

"Take another look round for it," her mother insists.

"But it's completely disappeared!" says the little girl.

"Don't get so upset!" replies her mother, trying to calm her down.

"Well, I am upset, because it's a mystery," protests Jenny. "I put it down on this table."

"Perhaps you're mistaken..." suggests her mother.

"I'm telling you no. I'm sure of it. I put it here on this table, and when I went to pick it up again it was gone: flown away, disappeared!"

"That is strange. It almost seems as though it did fly away." But even Jenny's mother doesn't realize that is exactly what did happen. Jenny's ribbon really did fly away, in the beak of a finch!

The cunning little bird had spotted the green velvet ribbon, and decided that it looked so soft, that it had to have it! The finch will tear it into little pieces for its nest. Birds sometimes build their nests out of the strangest and most unusual materials.

5 Vanilla and her new family

Yesterday, in Miss Emily's kitchen, a most unusual event took place. Vanilla, the cat, gave birth to three lovely kittens.

As soon as Clare heard about it, she decided that she wanted to go and see them.

She rushed out of the house to her neighbor's, and rang the doorbell.

"Good evening, Miss Emily, please may I see the kittens?"

"Of course, Clare, come in."

"Aren't they lovely!" exclaims the little girl at the sight of the newly-born kittens, who are curled up asleep, near their mother, in a large wicker basket.

One of the kittens is golden, like its mother, but with black stripes; another is also tawny, but of a lighter shade, and the third, the prettiest of them all, is pearly grey, with faint black stripes.

"Can I pat them?"

"No. Vanilla might think she has to protect them and she would scratch you. You can pat them when they are a bit bigger... and if your mother allows it, I'll even give you one as a present!"

"A kitten of my own?" asks Clare in amazement. "That would be the nicest present you could give me!"

6 The hares' special day

Today is a special day!

The sunrise casts a pink light over everything and the tall grass in the fields is shining with dew. Across the plowed fields, lots of straight lines of light green shoots have appeared; in the vegetable gardens, the parsley and sage are growing.

Today is a special day!

The trees in the woods are covered with new leaves, the bushes are bursting with tiny buds. The breeze whispers through the trees, and the air is sweet and filled with fragrance.

Today is a special day!

The chirping of swallows can be heard all around; from a farmhouse comes the crowing of a solitary rooster. From the top of a lime tree a lively twittering can be heard, and on the farmhouse roof the pigeons coo tenderly.

Do you want to know why this is such a special day?

It is because the handsome young buck hare from the woods and the lovely young doe hare from the grove of fir trees have become engaged!

To show the world how happy they are, the two hares race across the fields and leap in the most carefree way.

Today really is a special day!

7 The field mouse goes out at night

The sun has set; darkness slowly spreads through the woods. In the nests, the chirping and twittering dies down and the birds lower their heads into their ruffled feathers and prepare for sleep.

But not all the inhabitants of the woods feel like going to sleep. On the contrary, some of them wait for the night to fall, so that they can go out at last.

The country mouse is one example! Do you know the field mouse? If not, allow me to introduce him to you: take a good look! Two small, round ears,

large, lively, shiny eyes, like two tiny, black, marbles; a pointed nose, and elegant, long whiskers. The field mouse has grey-brown fur; paws with white marks on them; a short tail which is also thin and dark on the top, light underneath. This little, nocturnal rodent has a very friendly look about it, even if it sometimes damages crops.

As soon as it grows dark, the country mouse leaves its den of dry leaves and hurries out into the fields. The grass smells lovely, just right for a mouse; warm under its paws. Hop, hop, hop! The field mouse jumps swiftly along.

8 The badger comes home

A rustling of leaves awakens the robin redbreast that was sleeping in the center of a large bush. The little bird raises its head and looks around: it is almost dawn, and it will soon be light in the woods.

The robin spies a badger among the bushes on its way back from its long, nightly walk. It moves heavily along the path: plof, plof, plof, plof; then suddenly, it disappears into its well-concealed den.

"Until we meet again... badger friend!" sleepy robin thinks.

9 The squirrels find a new home

Good news! The two squirrels have found a new house at the top of the big fir tree. It is an old crows' nest, which was abandoned months ago. It is a very well-placed home: peaceful, with plenty of sunshine, and fresh air!

The two little squirrels don't waste any time and begin making the necessary repairs. First of all, using twigs, they strengthen the framework of their new home and round its edges. Then, to prevent drafts from coming through the walls, they line the nest with thin pieces of tree bark: then they fill it with soft moss, to keep it warm and comfortable.

To make it easy for them to enter their new home, the squirrels make a comfortable opening in one side of the nest. At the same time, they make another safety exit on the other side, to allow for escape in case of danger. You can never be too careful! Now it is ready. Our busy pair of squirrels didn't do all this work just for themselves, as you've probably guessed. They did it so that they would have a home for their future family!

10 The little rabbits jump around

As soon as the full moon appears in the sky, the seven little rabbits leave their burrow down in the roots of the old chestnut tree, and off they go – hop, hop, hop, hop! – towards the clearing, which is like daylight in the moon's white rays. The owl, a nocturnal bird, watches them arrive.

Now, in the bright moonlight, they are playfully leaping around on the sweet-smelling grass. They make twists and turns, they roll over each other and, most of all, they make high jumps. It almost seems as if they have springs in their long, back legs!

11 The tunnel-digging mole

"Oh no, not the mole again!" exclaims Matthew. "When is it going to stop digging its tunnels under here?"

It's a question for which there is no answer! The insect-eating mole, who, as a consequence, is called an insectivore, is guilty of making those piles of earth that have ruined Matthew's well-tended lawn. The mole is a tireless digger. It uses its front paws like shovels, and with its back ones it pushes out the loose earth. This is the way it finds its food.

12 Underneath a lettuce leaf

The fresh lettuce is growing very well in the vegetable garden: in the warm, spring sunshine the plants are growing more and more round, and they are opening up their wide, curvy leaves, all colored tender green.

Three butterflies are flying around close by. Everything seems calm and tranquil. But, if we have a look underneath a lettuce leaf, we discover a great deal of movement going on.

Underneath the delicate, pale green canopy, a tiny world is busily working away. A young snail with a yellow shell

with grey stripes is waving its two antennae. A fly is busy rubbing its two hairy legs together. Five ants are struggling along under the weight of some large grains of wheat. A shiny worm contracts and expands in never-ending gymnastics. There is also a tiny spider rushing about as if it is late, while a shiny golden beetle, which has fallen on its back, from an apple branch, waves its legs in the air. Last of all, a flock of greenflies is struggling up the underside of the leaf. As you can see, there is quite a crowd down there!

13 Introducing... the Country Mouse

My name is Country Mouse, which means that I come from the countryside. I dress in very plain clothes: red, with slight grey tones. I live in the middle of the fields, and to make my den I have to dig at least six holes and a multitude of tunnels!

I wander around a lot. I can run very fast and swim perfectly! I find climbing very tiring, however. I love the warmth, hate the rain, and like large families. I also have to admit that I have a very big appetite! But that's another story!

14 The surprise hidden in the stones

"I don't like this pile of stones," says Matthew's father, pointing at the pile of stones at the edge of the lawn.

"I'll take them away," offers Matthew, happy to be of help.

"But they're too heavy for you," says his father.

"No, no they're not. I'll move them one at a time. I'll load them into my wheelbarrow and take them to the edge of the road," insists Matthew.

"Go ahead then," says his father.

Matthew hurries off to get his wheelbarrow and starts to work. Stone after stone he puts into the wheelbarrow and, when it is full, he pushes it to the edge of the road.

But then, lifting a large flat stone, Matthew comes across a large, brown toad, staring up at him with its big protruding eyes.

"Oh, oh!" exclaims Matthew in surprise, and he rushes to tell his father. "There's a toad under that pile of stones!" says Matthew seriously. "And we certainly can't take away its home!"

"You're right," his father agrees.

So, the rest of the stones are left as a home for the toad and its family.

15 Waiting quietly for hedgehogs

Mark and Clare are keeping watch through the kitchen window. Each evening for a week, they have been putting a bowl of milk outside the window. They are hoping that a hedgehog will come along and drink it. Peter, their cousin, has told them that hedgehogs love milk, and he added: "With all that wood piled up near the orchard wall, and with all that honeysuckle, I am sure that somewhere in your garden you will have a hedgehog! It is a nice, little animal which loves quiet places, where it can hide, and, at the same time, eat little insects. Piles of leaves, stacks of wood, hedges, and bushes are all ideal places for it."

Mark and Clare believed what their cousin told them, and now they are waiting patiently inside the window.

Tonight, finally, they see first one shape, then another, appear out of the darkness, like prickly, round balls. There are two big hedgehogs who are snuffling their way towards the fresh milk. When they reach the bowl, they settle down to drink.

16 The water lilies are in bloom

Jane is spending a few days on vacation at her aunt's house, long days full of discoveries! The first discovery is her aunt's house itself, which is not like most other houses. It is an old, restored mill. It still has its huge wheel which, squeaking a bit, continues to turn, under the thrust of the water from the stream that flows beside the house.

Everyday her aunt takes Jane out on long walks. She shows her a lot of things that Jane would never have discovered by herself: the different trees, the flowers, the herbs which look similar, but each one is different from the others.

"There's the old willow. We're nearly there," says her aunt. "At the pond. Look!" Amid the rushes and the reeds in the pond they can see the reflection of water. "Where?" asks Jane.

"What a lot of yellow flowers!" exclaims Jane. "What are they called?" "They are water lilies. As you might guess from the name, they live in ponds and streams."

"It's so quiet and peaceful here," sighs Jane.

"Yes, now it is! But wait a while and you'll see a big change!" her aunt warns.

17 The seven, lively, little ducklings

Jane's aunt was right! So much happens in and around the pond! But there are very few witnesses to see what happens: at the most, a few flies, a little spider, a snail, because everything happens in the shelter of the reeds and the rushes in the pond.

About a month ago, a lovely, wild duck built her nest at this very spot. She chose this pond instead of the one where she was born. But what a long journey our wild duck has had to make to get here. Fortunately, she wasn't alone. She was accompanied by her proud, green-necked drake, with his magnificent emerald-colored plumage.

When she found the place she was looking for, she at once began building a comfortable nest out of leaves. Then she laid seven, pale green eggs in it, and immediately covered them with a thin layer of grass, so that they would be better hidden. The duck began to brood over them, all by herself. Every time she has to go away for a while she pulls out some of her warm, soft feathers, so that the eggs are kept as warm as possible.

One fine morning, tap, tap, tap, seven, lively, little ducklings break out of their eggs, almost at the same time. The seven ducklings are yellow and brown, their feathers all ruffled. At once they start squawking and moving all over the place, as if they want to leave the nest already. But the mother duck does not want them to leave. She spreads her warm, soft wings to shelter them from the cold.

18 The ducklings take their first swim

The ducklings were only born yesterday but, together with their mother, the wild duck, they are already going down to the banks of the pond.

The new-born ducklings are very funny! They wobble on their webbed feet and follow the duck with small, cautious, uncertain steps, bumping into things as they go.

And yet, as soon as they reach the edge of the water, splash, they all jump in. And, surprise, surprise, they start swimming right away. They are natural swimmers who do not need lessons!

19 The jumping competition

Flip, flap, flop! Three brief splashes break the quiet surface of the pond; then everything is silent again. There is not a breath of wind; the reeds are standing up straight and still. Flip, flap, flop! The strange noise is heard again. Where is it coming from?

Jane tries to find out. But nothing is moving on the pond this afternoon. The ducks have moved away to where the clean water is flowing, among the water cress plants. And yet, flip, flap, flop, the strange sound is heard again. And, what's more, there is now, a sort of muffled croaking sound. Jane laughs to herself because she realizes what it is. It is the little, green frogs, taking part in a high-jump competition. They are making all the noises. In a sheltered part of the pond, well-hidden behind a curtain of reeds and the leaves of the water lilies, the frogs are making mighty leaps. With one kick of their elastic back legs, the frogs leap up into the air, then they dive, flip, back into the water. They make another jump, flap! and yet another, flop! And, in between all these jumps and splashes, there's lots of croaking!

20 The moorhen's water walk

Jane has come back to the pond, and, while her aunt sits under the willow tree, the little girl approaches the water's edge. She huddles down amid the reeds, and, hidden there, she waits to see what will happen. Suddenly Jane sees a moorhen. To her great surprise, the lovely, dark-colored bird, with its bright red beak, seems to be jumping on its long thin legs from one lily to another. It moves so swiftly and lightly, it gives the impression that it is walking on the water!

21 Three shadows at dawn

It is dawn. A soft, grey mist rises up from the calm waters of the pond. This mist, as thin as a veil, wraps itself around the reeds, drifts in among the branches of the old, willow tree, and touches the edges of the pond. Everything looks calm and mysterious...

Suddenly, from out of the pearly-grey haze, the outlines appear of some slender figures. Let's see if we can recognize them.

"The largest one, with the long, thin legs, is a heron!"

"That's right. So it is. It can also be recognized by its long neck and its very long beak."

Another shadow takes shape among the reeds. This one is stiff and its strong neck points upwards.

"Only a bittern stands like that!"

"Yes, it is the main characteristic of that lovely bird!"

Now a third outline appears just above the water line: its neck is slender and on its head are two tufts of shiny feathers.

"I know that one. It's a great crested grebe. Grebes have paddle-shaped feet to help them to swim."

"Yes that is what it is. Now we will have to come back for a better look at them during the daytime."

22 A frog moves to the city

Jane has returned home after a lovely vacation at her aunt's house. Do you want to know what she brought back as a present for her brother Andrew?

"A picture of the mill?"

"No!"

"A big stone from the stream?"

"Not that either!"

"A cake from her aunt?"

"No, not that either. She brought him a frog; alive, of course! A big green frog."

For the journey, Jane put the frog in a glass jar, but now she has to find a good place for it to live. Andrew immediately thinks of the goldfish bowl and rushes off to get it.

So that the little frog will feel more at home, Jane puts some white gravel and some pebbles in the glass bowl. Then the two children carefully put the frog in its new home. It doesn't seem too unhappy, or at all afraid... In fact, hop! It takes a big jump out and lands on Andrew's shoulder!

"It's all cold and slimy!" he exclaims.

Whether it wants to or not, back the frog goes into the bowl!

"You'll have to accept living in a bowl for a while, my little friend," Jane says to it.

23 How to identify ducks

Is it very difficult to distinguish between one kind of duck and another?

Of course, you can tell a mallard, with a dark green head, from a teal, with a reddish head. But, only when you glimpse the shiny, colored feathers on the back edges of its wings when in flight, are you sure of the species.

Look at the green-necked mallard in flight: the back edges of its wings are violet-blue.

Now look at the teal flying over; the trailing edges of its wings are green with black reflections.

24 So much for ducklings

The ducklings in the pond are now a few days old, and they have already grown a great deal. These funny, little, yellow balls of fluff waddle around the plants by the water's edge. They flop into the water in the pond. They are champion swimmers, and, most of all, they eat all day long, from morning to night.

I don't think you will share their tastes, but I'd like to list all the food that these little web-footed creatures seek out so diligently.

First of all, the ducklings love the tiny freshwater fish that, with one peck of their beaks, they dig out of the muddy bed of the pond. Then, there are the tender water plants, so fresh and succulent. Even the tadpoles are tasty morsels, and, sometimes, on rare occasions, the ducklings even manage to catch a frog!

There is so much tasty food for ducks in the pond! There are tender mosquitoes to be caught in flight. With a bit of luck, the odd, absent-minded spider can be caught, lazily floating on a leaf. Even an elegant dragonfly can be grabbed out of the air during one of its flights. On rainy days, there are also snails. So, have a day full of good meals, ducklings!

25 Two special ducks

"I am a garganey, one of the smallest of all wild ducks. If you want to recognize me, look at my head: it is light brown, with a white line like an eyebrow on each side. I love flying fast, and I glide, as light as a feather, across the surface of the pond. When I am looking for a mate, my croaking sounds just like the chirping of a cricket."

"I am a shoveler. I get my name from my big heavy bill, which I shovel through the water and mud in search of food. Don't you admire the blue patches on the front of my wings!"

26 A fine, floating nest

A floating home, a nest built on the water. Which bird has this idea? It is the beautiful, freshwater bird, the great crested grebe, with a long, white neck, and two horns of feathers on its head.

A pair of grebes put together innumerable pieces of reeds, rushes and water plants, one by one, to form a kind of floating platform, their nest. The female then lays her blue-white eggs. There she calmly broods over them, rocked by the gentle movement of the water.

27 Danger in the marshes

The marshland is so set apart and peaceful that it often seems enchanted. But just as there are wicked witches in fairy tales, there are also some animals in the marshes it is best to avoid!

The coot, for example, is not as sweet as it looks. Of course, it has beautiful, shiny, black plumage, but the white on its forehead and its beak does not make it look very friendly! Furthermore, this water bird shrieks and wails so loudly that nothing wants to get too close to it!

Then there is the polecat, another creature to be wary of. This mammal has shiny, rusty-red fur, a small pointed muzzle with white marks, and short paws with long, strong nails. It is a fearsome hunter with a huge appetite, ready to devour small mammals, fish, frogs, and even large, strong birds, like ducks.

Over the marshes and ponds there also hangs the threat of the birds of prey, like the marsh harrier, a truly dangerous hawk. When it hovers over the reeds, you can be sure that its intention is to sink its claws into a poor little water-vole or frog.

28 Rocked to sleep on the water

How pretty the grebe's new-born chicks are. They have soft feathers which form a striped coat! From time to time, their mother puts them on her back so that they don't get too tired swimming.

How does she do it? It's easy! She is an excellent swimmer, so she sinks under the water, leaving just her back sticking out. Then the youngsters can climb up onto her soft feathers, so that both the mother grebe and her young can gently rock on the water.

29 The patient fisherman

The midday sun shines down on the water, turning the surface a golden color. Along the water's edge, a heron is walking with measured steps. It almost seems to be counting its steps, because it moves so carefully on its long, thin legs. It takes a few steps forward, then slowly it retraces its steps. Suddenly it raises one of its legs and stands motionless on the other one.

What is it waiting for in that odd position? A visitor? No, the heron is a solitary bird, and it has very few visitors. Maybe it is sleeping on its feet? Not at all; on the contrary, it is wide-awake and alert: it is stalking a fish!

Like all the best fishermen, it knows how to wait patiently. It can stand still in such a posture, for up to two hours. This gives us the chance to have a good look at its long beak, and its long, bent neck, which it folds back against its shoulders when it is flying, and at its large, black-tipped wings.

But we don't have the time to wait and see what small fish the heron is waiting for. So, goodbye, and happy fishing!

30 A noisy, sunset gathering

A light breeze gently bends the reeds in the water and the smooth surface of the pool is broken by tiny waves, which reflect the last golden-red rays of the setting sun. Returning from their hunting expeditions, the various inhabitants of the marsh and the pond settle onto the water with a constant rustling of wings and spraying of water.

It seems that they are all telling each other about their day, catching up on the latest news. The air is filled with quacks, chirps and squawks! The divers are the noisiest of all; they croak, squawk, and call out. Some of the ducks let out shrill noises, while, in the distance, a solitary bittern, hidden among the reeds, sends out loud booms which sound like foghorns.

This evening the noise goes on longer than usual. The green-headed mallard drake has come back to visit his family. The ducklings are all admiring his lovely plumage, and his bright green neck! Now the moon has risen. It is time for birds to put their heads under their wings and go to sleep. Tomorrow is another day.

1 The lily of the valley

Today is a school holiday. Mark and Clare run off into the woods near their garden.

"This way!" Mark directs.

The two children move deeper into the woods, their eyes on the ground, almost as if they are looking for mushrooms.

"Here they are!"

"Ah yes, here too!"

Still wrapped in their spiral of wide leaves, the first, white flowers of the sweet-smelling lily of the valley are appearing. It is the flower which symbolizes the month of May.

2 A difficult choice for an artist

In the house, there are lilies of the valley everywhere! The pretty little bunches of flowers, arranged so lovingly in vases, make Clare want to draw a picture of them. But which will she choose? There are wild lilies of the valley, picked in the woods, with half-closed flowers, some white, some pale green. They give off a delicate, fresh scent which brings memories of walks in the shadowy woods. Clare's mother has arranged them in a glass vase.

But there are also lilies of the valley which have been grown in greenhouses. They have long, slender stalks and perfect, little, white flower bells which hang at regular intervals. Unfortunately, though, they have no scent. Her mother has put the greenhouse-grown lilies of the valley in an elegant porcelain vase.

With her pencil poised in the air, Clare hesitates. She doesn't know which ones to choose. The wild lilies of the valley, picked in the woods, are more charming in their fragile simplicity, leaves wrapped around the flowers as if to protect them. The greenhouse lilies of the valley have more elegant shapes, a little rigid, but very precise, so they are easier to draw. If you were an artist, which would you choose?

3 The ladybugs' climbing competition

Two pretty little ladybugs, who have awakened from their winter sleep, have decided to stretch their legs, and make a difficult climb! One of them is golden yellow with six tiny, black dots; the other is bright red, with just two black dots on its back. They are at the bottom of a lily of the valley stalk, the tallest lily in the bunch, in the middle of the vase. Which of the two ladybugs will be first to the top?

The smallest, the yellow one, starts off very well and moves in short bursts, as if he has a motor inside him. His feet move in precise, tireless movements.

The red ladybug moves more slowly. At times, it stops, it probes with its antennae, then it continues climbing.

On the lily of the valley, there are seven little, white, bell-like flowers. The speedy, little yellow ladybug suddenly changes direction, moving off to the left. It ends its climb on the sixth flower. The red ladybug, on the other hand, carries on straight up to the top flower. Slow and steady wins the race!

4 Not as warm as it seems

Elizabeth is singing softly to herself as she looks through her closet for her flowery, cotton dress, the one she wore last year on her birthday. For the coming months she can put away her heavy, woollen dresses, corduroy pants, and sweaters.

It is the month of May and it feels like summer. Elizabeth eventually finds her flowery dress at the bottom of a neatly folded pile of clothes. It seems a little short, but she puts it on anyway.

She is still singing to herself when she goes skipping out into the garden.

Then she gives a little shiver. Although the sun is shining, and the air is cool, goose bumps suddenly appear on Elizabeth's arms. Maybe it is not yet warm enough for summer clothes, but Elizabeth likes her brightly colored, summer dress so much. Anyway she decides that if she feels cold, all she has to do is to jump rope to keep warm!

5 Good morning, larks

Jenny goes to the mailbox four times a day, including Sundays, but not to get the mail. She goes to visit her new friends; 'the lark family of the full moon.'

Jenny calls them this because their eggs were hatched on the night of the full moon. What a surprise she had next morning; and also a small disappointment! The five spotted eggs were gone, and there were five little birds in their place. They were very ugly, all bald and wrinkly, with their eyes closed.

She felt sorry for them, because they were so small and defenseless. Now Jenny thinks they are much prettier. Thanks to the insect morsels their parents give them all day long, the little chicks have grown, their eyes are wide open and now their bodies are covered in soft feathers.

So now you can see why Jenny enjoys spending so much time by the mailbox, watching the little larks. There is always something happening in the busy nest. As soon as one of the parents arrive, the little chicks thrust their wide-open beaks up in the air.

6 A never-ending task

It is easy to say: "How lovely the baby larks are!" But it would be better to say "well done" to the tireless parents, who are out hunting insects from morning 'til night to feed their ever-hungry young. Their mother and father have no sooner finished feeding them a spider, than off they fly again to catch some insects on the apple trees, then back and forth again to catch a butterfly, a worm, a caterpillar... What an endless job of work! And isn't it nice to see those gaping little beaks!

7 Five new-born squirrels

One! Two! Three! Four! Five!

Five new-born squirrels! What a big family! Luckily their far-sighted parents have prepared a nice big nest.

The little squirrels did not hatch out of eggs, like the birds; but they were born live from their mother, like a cat has kittens, and a dog has puppies, just like little mice and other mammals.

Do you want to know what new-born squirrels look like? Well, to be honest, they do not look very attractive. First of all, they are very small; they don't weigh more than one ounce each! Completely naked, they are born without fur, and they don't even have a tail. They are born with their eyes closed, and they don't open them for thirty days.

They are very small and delicate, but as far as their mother is concerned, they are the finest baby squirrels in the world! She keeps them warm in her thick fur and feeds them with her milk. She takes care of them all by herself! The father squirrel goes away the same day they are born: he moves out of the nest to leave room for the new family.

8 The nature detectives

"When you go into the woods, how do you know what are your chances of seeing a squirrel?" Clare asks her older cousin Peter.

"It's easy. All you have to do is play a certain game."

"What game?" asks Clare.

"A detective game," answers her cousin. The little girl looks at him in astonishment, but Peter continues, unperturbed. "Come on," he says, "I'll show you how it works!"

A few minutes later, the two children are in the woods. "Look at the ground carefully," advises Peter. "We have to look with a detective's eyes for signs of the squirrels passing."

"But with all these plants and undergrowth, it is impossible to see a squirrel's footprints."

"You're right: we have to look for other clues. First of all, we will take a close look under the fir and larch trees. They are the trees that the squirrels like the most. Here, look," Peter murmurs, picking up a nibbled pine cone, "these are the left-overs of a meal." They both look up, in time to see a magnificent squirrel climbing rapidly to the top of the fir tree... The detective game works!

9 A wedding feast in the moonlight

The moon is shining in the sky, a friendly, bright moon. The hare from the chestnut grove and his new wife are racing happily down the slope, crossing the fields with huge leaps on their way to the best vegetable garden in the village, where they plan to have a wedding feast!

They are very selective in their choice; only young carrots, tender lettuce, and radishes which melt in the mouth. But then a dog barks. "Come on, we have to run!" The moon helpfully hides behind a cloud. This will make the hares' escape easier!

10 An adventurous bicycle ride

Mark and Clare have been allowed to go out on their bikes. "Don't go too fast! Don't go too far! Come home early!" Their mother cautions them.

"Yes, mother," the children promise and off they go.

They have agreed to ride to the open space by the woods, and they set off along a packed earth path. They pedal hard, enjoying the sound of the wind whistling all around them. "We are going really fast!" they both think...

They ride past the cornfields and along the edge of the dark woods of pine.

Mark, who is in the lead, suddenly hears a long call coming from behind him: *"cucuu... cucuu..."* He turns around and says to his sister: "What is it?"

"Nothing," answers Clare. "I didn't say a word!"

"Stop fooling around," says Mark. "You made a noise: *cucuu, cucuu.* Why?"

"I'm telling you I never even opened my mouth," says Clare crossly.

"Fine. I believe you," grumbles Mark, who can't bear being made fun of by his sister.

The two children continue riding side by side, through the tall trees bordering the road.

"Cucuu, cucuu!" Again they hear it. Mark and Clare look at each other. "Well, who is calling us then?" Mark wonders, a bit worried. "How strange!" murmurs Clare, nervously. "Let's go back!" And she turns her bicycle around and races back in the direction of the village. Her brother follows her. He doesn't like mysterious sounds from the woods either, especially when they come from the dark, mysterious woods of pine trees.

11 The story of the cuckoo

The day after their bicycle outing, Clare and Mark ask their cousin Peter about the *cucuu* sound. He tells them that they were hearing the cuckoo's song.

"The cuckoo is a large, grey bird, with a long tail, and short, yellow legs. When you hear its piercing call ringing through the woods, then you can be sure that the spring has really come! But the cuckoo's call also frightens other birds, because it means trouble for them!"

"What trouble?" asks Clare.

Peter explains: "This large bird never builds its own nest. When it is time for the female cuckoo to lay her eggs, she begins to fly over the trees in the woods looking for the nests of other birds. If she spies a lark's nest on a lime tree, she will settle on a nearby branch. Then, when the parent larks leave, the cuckoo pushes one of the eggs out and lets it fall to the ground."

"How terrible!" exclaims Mark.

Peter continues: "In its place, the cuckoo lays one of her own eggs, large and white with red spots. It is actually the same color as the lark's eggs, only larger. When it has done this, the cuckoo flies away. The larks return home to find a shattered egg at the bottom of the tree, and an enormous cuckoo's egg in the nest!"

"Poor things..." says Clare, full of indignation. "So what do the birds do then? I bet they throw out the big, strange egg!"

"I'll tell you the rest of the story later," replies Peter.

12 Where is the missing hedgehog?

"Only one hedgehog turned up for milk this evening," Clare tells her brother.

"Perhaps the other one will come after you've gone to bed," suggests Mark.

After the first evening that the two hedgehogs came to drink the milk out of the bowl by the window, Mark and Clare have kept watch faithfully.

Each evening, they see the two, waddling shapes approach the house, apparently with no fear. The two little hedgehogs always drink all the milk, not leaving a drop. Then they go away,

letting out little grunts of satisfaction. Clare would love to go outside and get a closer look at them, maybe even touch them.

"You would only scare them, and they would prick you," her brother always tells her. "But one little hedgehog is now alone, poor thing," says Clare. "Let's hope the other one isn't sick."

13 The hedgehogs' happy event

In the small shelter, in the hollow between two stones in the wall surrounding the vegetable garden, the mother hedgehog has given birth to four babies, each one more charming than the other.

Now we know why one hedgehog didn't show up for the milk last night!

The little hedgehog has prepared a bed of leaves for her young, and now she is watching them proudly. They are like little balls, covered in soft, white needles. Their eyes are still closed and they have no hair on their faces.

14 A walk after the rain

It has just stopped raining and a snail is preparing to go out for a look around. We don't know what it is thinking, but, from the happy way it is moving, we can imagine.

"Oh what fun to go out after the rain! The grass is fresh and damp, and you can slide over it so easily. The earth has a lovely smell, which gives you an appetite. Between the branches, the spiders' webs look like decorations. They are decorated with dew drops that shine like huge diamonds."

"As I pass, the tall grass gives me a warm, stimulating shower! And all the birds, who had taken shelter during the storm, have now come out to start singing again."

"Yes, I definitely like going out for a walk after a heavy rainfall! When I am happy, I stick my antennae out as far as possible and move easily up the slope. In these conditions, I can even beat the snails' speed record: fifty-five yards per hour! And my lovely shell-house feels as light as a feather. There's nothing better in the world than going for a walk after the rain!"

15 The fieldmice run a race

Here they come! There they go! Hop, hop, hop!

With long, elastic hops the fieldmice move along the trail of soft moss. The trail passes through the sweet-smelling hawthorn bush; it goes up the steep slope, covered in buttercups; it disappears in a tuft of tall ferns; and then it reappears right in the middle of an open space. The trail continues, climbing past the knotted roots of the big fir tree. The fieldmice move along the side of the stream. Then they all sink into the tall grass; and the race continues merrily across the fields.

16 The cuckoo's story continues

Clare can hardly wait for Peter to continue the story of the cuckoo, which he began a few days ago.

"When she has gotten over her surprise, the mother bird realizes that this big, strange egg needs her care, her warmth, just like her own two remaining eggs. And so, ruffling out her feathers, she patiently begins to sit on all the eggs, both her own and the intruder. Ten days later, two little larks are born. But, instead of dedicating all her energy to feeding them, the mother continues to sit on the other big egg."

"At last, a few days later, the little cuckoo also breaks out of its shell. In contrast to the others, it looks enormous, with a huge head and two big eyes."

"The cuckoo moves and complains! It is hungry!" The parents fly far and wide to find food for it, but the cuckoo is impossible to satisfy. It even steals food from the other two babies. It knocks into them and pecks them, because it is always so hungry.

"As it eats so much, the young cuckoo grows very quickly, and the nest soon becomes too small for it..."

17 Cuckoos have their uses

"Then what?" asks Clare sounding worried.

"Then," Peter continues, "by squirming, and making sure it gets all the attention, the cuckoo pushes the two little birds out of the nest!"

"Oh, that's horrible!" cries Clare indignantly. "Don't go on. I don't want to hear this horrible story any more!"

"Wait, wait till the end," replies Peter. "You have to realize that it is not so simple... The parents feed the young cuckoo until it is capable of flying off by itself..."

"I hate this story, and I hate cuckoos as well!" insists Clare.

"No, you mustn't hate these birds," her cousin Peter says seriously. "Without them the woods would die away, because there wouldn't be any more trees. The other birds would not be able to build their nests, and they would also die out!"

"How come?" asks Clare, curious and suspicious.

"The cuckoos, and only the cuckoos, eat the big, furry caterpillars which devour the leaves and bark of all types of trees. In this way, they save the whole woods!"

"Oh well, if that's the case..." admits Clare, grudgingly!

18 Clare chooses her kitten

Vanilla's three kittens have grown quickly. They have become more confident and playful: they are enchanting.

Miss Emily has told Clare that she can go and choose her kitten. This is a very happy day for Clare. The young girl looks at the three little balls of fluff, and finally she chooses the white one with orange and grey markings.

"I'd like this one," she declares, pointing at the kitten she has chosen.

19 Clare's kitten, Pudding

What is the first thing you have to do when you are given an animal for a present? Give it a name, of course!

So, as she is stroking the kitten's soft fur, Clare says: "I'll call you... I'll call you... Pudding!"

Her mother approves. "That's a good choice. It is a name which suits this kitten perfectly!"

The second thing you must do when you get an animal, is to prepare a proper bed for it, where it can sleep. So Clare gets a wicker basket, puts an old, soft cushion into it, and then she places it at the end of the corridor, near her room. Then she prepares a box of sawdust. "This is your litterbox," she tells the kitten, picking it up, gently but firmly, by the neck. "You mustn't dirty the house, but come here every time. Understand?"

Then Clare gets two dishes, one for milk and one for food. "Well, now you've got all you need, little Pudding. Welcome to our house!"

20 The first signs of trouble

Pudding seems very happy in his new home. He has spent a peaceful night in his soft basket. But now he is feeling a bit restless; and so he decides to go out exploring.

He goes out through the half-open door to Clare's bedroom. "I'll explore under the bed," he thinks. "Oh look, here's something interesting! A nice, blue slipper: it seems just perfect to sharpen my claws on!"

21 A host of happy butterflies

This morning the garden seems to be quivering all over. The air is unusually light. It almost looks as if the flowers are about to take off, or as if little pieces of colored cloth are floating everywhere.

What is going on? Is it a dream? No, it is a butterfly invasion. These insects make the garden brighter, with their fantastic, unpredictable patterns of flight. The delicate colors and the precious lacework of their wings are a joy to behold. Welcome to our garden, lovely friends!

22 The lost butterfly

A butterfly has come into the house. I heard a small tap on the windowpane and then a rapid beating of wings as it fluttered in confusion. Then I was able to make out its lovely colors: red, purple, golden brown: it was a wonderful sight.

What a beautiful visitor! But how frantic it was! It continued to flutter against the window, confused by the transparency of that thin barrier. The poor little thing was desperately trying to get back out into the garden among its scented flowers. Back again it went to tap against the glass. Stunned, it tried yet again, and then made still another attempt.

"You'll end up damaging your lovely, delicate wings. Wait, I'll come and open the window for you. There you are, pretty butterfly. Now you are free," said Clare.

But the gorgeous, iridescent insect finally seemed to have gained confidence in its new surroundings. Fluttering in its never-ending acrobatics, it flew low over an armchair in the living room, and then rested for a little while on a velvet curtain. It hovered in front of the mirror and then flew rings around the lampshade. It seemed as if the beautiful, little butterfly had no desire to leave!

23 The ladybug's defense

The sun is shining, the air is warm and perfect for going for a walk. The ladybug shakes its tiny wings out of its shell; it then spreads them out and flies off towards the branch of an apple tree. How lovely it is to fly among these lovely, fresh, green leaves.

But, all of a sudden, a bird blocks its path! The ladybug is terrified of ending up inside the bird's beak. But did you know that, when it is frightened, this tiny insect gives off a horrible smell? So the bird decides that it is better to fly away than to remain anywhere near such a bad odor!

24 Pudding the troublemaker

One thing is for sure: Pudding, Clare's brown and white kitten, is going to grow up to be a great explorer!

He has only been in his new house for a few days and he has already been into every nook and cranny!

Clare only manages to catch an occasional glimpse of him, before he goes straight off to explore somewhere else.

"Where's Pudding?" asks Clare as soon as she arrives home from school.

"He shouldn't be far away," replies her mother. "I saw him in the hallway a few minutes ago."

Clare goes into her bedroom to put down her school bag.

"What a mess!" she exclaims when she sees the wastepaper basket overturned on the floor and the contents spread all over the place. And her slippers are upside down in the middle of the floor again!

So Clare goes back out into the hall to find her naughty cat. But, suddenly, a thought occurs to her and she goes back into the room. Just as she expected, the wastepaper basket has moved its position while she was out!

But it is nothing to worry about, because – would you believe it – that silly, little kitten is rolling inside the basket, just as if it were on one of the rides at the fair.

25 A rustling in the dark

Maggie awakes to a persistent, rustling sound, and remembers that she is in her cousin Sophie's house in the country.

"I must have been dreaming," she says to herself, turning over in the bed to try and get back to sleep.

But the rustling sound goes on, even louder than before. It is a soft sound, like paper being crumpled. By this time, Maggie is wide-awake.

She is not an easily frightened, little girl, but she would really like to know where that noise is coming from!

So she starts to feel around for the light switch. It is not easy to find in a room which is not familiar to her, but at last her hand comes across it. The light illuminates the whole room. At first, Maggie does not notice anything. While her eyes are getting used to the light, the rustling continues. The noise obsesses her!

"I don't see any mice," Maggie thinks. "And it can't be a bird, or even a little bat. So what can it be then?"

A few moments later, Maggie finally discovers the source of the mysterious, persistent rustling. There are two small moths, all grey and furry, caught inside the paper lampshade.

26 Alone in the woods!

"Dawn is coming earlier and earlier," thinks the little rabbit. "I haven't finished my night rounds yet and the sky is already beginning to grow light. Today, my rabbit friends will be having fun playing in the clover fields. I prefer to go and explore the woods. In a few, great leaps, I can get to the first trees. Look how thick and tall they are! See how dark it is in here! Suddenly, I can't see the sky anymore. And how quiet it is... so this is what it's like in the woods."

"Well, I must confess I'm a little frightened, so I'd better leave."

27 Look out!... the wild boar is coming!

Yes, the forest, with its tall trees and mysterious, dark places, can be a bit scary. It is like stepping into a different world, unknown and secret.

There is no bright bustle of the open woodlands, with the constant sound of birds singing, the humming of insects, the quick, sudden movements of little rabbits and mice, and the soft murmur of the breeze among the trees. In the forest, silence seems to reign supreme!

But there are animals in the forest. It seems to be completely deserted, which is comforting in one sense, but worrying at the same time. It some-

times happens that the silence is suddenly broken by the cracking of branches, by a heavy thudding and a rough grunting. What on earth is making that noise?

The ground begins to tremble under heavy blows and the sound comes closer. All of a sudden, out of the trees an animal appears, large, bristly, with dark fur, and bloodshot eyes, with strong sharp tusks and a thick neck. It is a wild boar, three hundred and fifty pounds of it! Then after a few minutes, the silence returns to the forest: the "hurricane" has passed!

28 The little boar's awakening

It's impossible to go on sleeping! All around, its brothers keep moving about. The little boar would have liked to carry on sleeping in its warm, muddy, comfortable bed!

But it's almost impossible to get any peace, with all the grunting and endless snorting going on, not to mention the pokes it keeps getting in the muzzle, and all the other disturbances.

And now look, the mother boar is getting up. This is no time to be lying around anymore. We have to follow her. One, two, three, away! Off we go!

29 A line of little boars

The moonlight filters in through the high branches of the birch trees and lights up the silvery trunks, arranged in long rows.

Suddenly, in the light of the moon, a strange procession comes into sight. At the front is a female boar with a long muzzle; and behind the sow are seven little boars, all in a line, pushing against each other. They look very comical with their striped coats!

They are very lively and playful little boar cubs, as they bite each other's ears, and see which one can make the loudest noise!

30 Whose lovely red tail is that?

This morning, the sun is shining down on the opening in the big, shady forest.

But something is moving at the edge of the woods. What is that, shining in the spring sun? It looks like a thick tuft, red in color, waving above the long grass.

I can see now that it's a tail! And I have even guessed who it belongs to! What about you? Have you guessed yet?

Well, let me tell you that it belongs to an animal with a round head, slanting eyes and a long sharp muzzle. Now have you guessed? If I go on to tell you that it has russet fur, that its legs are thin, and that it is light-footed and sharp-eyed... then would you know who I am talking about? Not yet? Don't worry. I'll give you some more clues. It has a reputation for being very clever, even cunning.

As for its taste in food, it is very varied. It is just as happy to eat mice and rabbits, as little birds and frogs, and it loves fruit. But what it loves most of all are the nice, fat chickens in the henhouse, and given half a chance, it will steal one. This time you must have guessed the answer! Of course, it's the cunning fox.

31 A brave, little fox

"It's such a lovely day outside. I'm getting very bored staying here in the den," sighs the little fox, with its lovely, pointed ears.

It is very young, only one month old, with grey fur and a tail that still has to grow.

The fox cub's little brothers are safely asleep inside their den, while their mother is out getting some food. "Sleepy heads! I'm going out for a walk!" decides the brave, little fox. And with tiny leaps, it makes its way out onto the unknown path...

1 The fox family

When the mother fox, the vixen, comes back to the den, there is great excitement. She announces her arrival with a quiet yelp which has all the fox cubs instantly on their feet. They rush out happily to meet her.

Cheerfully, they leap and jump all over her. They bound around, falling over each other and then quickly getting up on their feet again. Eventually they nuzzle up to her to drink her milk. They are only little cubs and still need their mother's milk. The mother fox lets them drink as long as they need to; then she sends them away.

Then it is time to play. With gentle shoves of her muzzle, the vixen rolls her cubs over one by one. Meanwhile they are all biting each other playfully. The fox cubs never get tired of all this attention from her. They even roll over on their backs in the hope that she will scratch their tummies!

Today, the family is especially happy, because the father, the dog fox, has arrived as well.

2 A good hiding place

A new-born deer, a fawn, is lying hidden among the thick leaves of the woods. Although it is all alone, it is unafraid.

It is not even sad, because it knows that its mother will be along soon. It is not bored either because there are so many things to look at; the lovely fern waving in the breeze; the pine cone half-sunk into the moss; a caterpillar moving along a bramble leaf; and best of all there is that great spider's web strung between two springy, birch branches. The spider climbs up and down and backwards and forwards on its intricate web. The little deer makes a tiny movement on its soft bed of leaves; it shows its long, thin legs and a smooth reddish fur with white spots.

Suddenly, there is a rainstorm!

The bush where the mother deer gave birth to it is so thick that it even protects the fawn from the rain, and the warm bed of leaves stays completely dry. All around the rain falls heavily, and the little deer listens to the music it plays on the leaves, tapping against the roots and drumming on the path. The fawn is happy to be in its shelter.

3 The mother deer returns

The branches are pushed aside delicately, their rustling can only just be heard, but the newly born deer cub awakens instantly. Then it sees its mother, a beautiful doe, looking down at it. She pushes her way into the well-protected hiding place and lies down beside her baby.

Then she gives it a good licking over. Afterwards she nudges it to stand up. The tiny little animal sways on its thin legs, but soon it will be more sure-footed. Finally, it finds its balance and stands ready to follow its mother.

4 The roe deer's wonderful leap

The natural science teacher has organized a trip into the forest for his pupils, so that they can study nature first hand.

The children are dressed as the teacher has instructed: first of all, comfortable shoes, suitable for crossing over streams or muddy patches, or for walking over slippery grass: and then, of course, a knapsack, which contains a snack, some dry clothes, a map of the area, a compass: and, last but not least, a notebook to write down all their observations, and maybe even make some sketches.

The children are divided into groups of three. One of these is made up of Luke, Sandy, and John. It must be said that they are not the most enthusiastic of the children. They are wondering what could be of interest for them to see in the woods.

All of a sudden, right in front of them, a roe deer crosses their path in a single bound and disappears again. The three boys are speechless, stunned by such beauty and strength. They would be ready to search the whole forest, in order to see a sight like that again!

5 The mighty shape in the moonlight

Tonight, the moonlight creates magical shadows in the forest. They appear and disappear in the light of the moon, which is occasionally hidden by a passing cloud. But that great outline down there in the clearing is definitely not being caused by the light of the moon! The shape has a majestic head, crowned by spreading antlers, a thick neck, a straight back and strong legs. There is no doubt about it, it is a great male deer, a stag.

As we watch, it begins to roar, the sound rising and falling through the forest.

6 Perfume and magic in the country air

As soon as he got out of the car, Max, the basset hound, immediately discovered that there was something extraordinary in the country air. He was beside himself with excitement. He leapt in the grass impatiently, with his nose quivering in the air. He sniffed the wind and all the unusual smells, so unlike those in the city.

Max could feel that he was about to make new discoveries and he wagged his tail like mad. Catherine called him; but he didn't even hear her. Max, was too busy breathing in the fresh, country air, which was filled with so many promises.

7 Max, the basset hound, makes a new friend

When a city dog comes to the country it has to get to know both the new surroundings and the inhabitants.

The garden and the house, where our friend the basset has come with his mistress, is the undisputed territory of a fox-terrier called Skip, a bad-tempered, constantly agitated dog. Skip has already spotted the newcomer and is looking him over from nose to tail in a very superior manner.

Max, who is used to meeting lots of dogs on the sidewalks in the city, is surprised and offended at receiving such an unfriendly greeting. So he turns his back on Skip and goes off into the garden, where he soon becomes confused. No tuft of grass, no stone, nothing is familiar to him. Should he go to the right? Should he go to the left? Or should he go straight?

Then he comes across a little, green-painted, wooden house. He would like to go in, but Skip rushes up, barking; "This is my house, my home!" But then Skip's attitude changes. He wags his tail: "You can come in and see it if you want..."

Max is amazed. Skip has a house all to himself! He did not think that country dogs would be so fortunate!

8 Max and the cow

Since he's come to live in the country, what Max likes best is being able to run about freely at any time of the day. By now, he has come to know every corner of the garden, although he stops short at the big tree.

This morning, however, while he is bounding along the fence which marks the border of the farm, he comes face to face with a huge cow. Confronted by such a giant, Max feels very small. He decides that there is nothing else to do but run away as fast as his legs can carry him!

9 Discovering the farmyard animals

From down in the pen at the bottom of the garden, there comes a constant clucking, quacking and honking from the farmyard animals.

Catherine is very excited. For the first time she can see lots of animals that she has only known from pictures in books up until now. She likes to look at them one by one, and she studies them from head to foot, or rather from their beaks to their feet.

Beatrix, her little friend who lives in the country, is amazed by Catherine's excitement. While Beatrix likes the animals just as much, she cannot understand how they can be of such interest to Catherine.

"Oh, aren't they lovely!" exclaims Catherine, when she spies some fluffy little chicks trying to push their way under the wings of a hen.

"Oh, and aren't those ducks funny" she says, laughing at them waddling along.

"Oh, look at that beautiful tail!" she exclaims at the sight of the long, blue-green feathers which the rooster is proudly showing off, to a chorus of clucks from a group of admiring hens.

"Oh, what bright feathers those geese have," cries Catherine, as she spots two handsome, long-necked geese wandering past.

"This one looks as though he's all dressed up in his best suit. I've never seen anything like it," yells Catherine, when she sees a magnificent, male turkey puffing out its feathers.

The little city girl is delighted by every one of the farmyard animals. But all these loud cries of pleasure are not very pleasing to Max. The poor basset feels left out, forgotten. He is jealous of all these strange and wonderful birds which are as new to him as they are to Catherine. With his ears down, Max slinks off.

10 The butterfly chase

Max's good mood returns very quickly, as he goes running in the fields again. It is fun to go chasing after the butterflies, like that pretty, little, bright yellow one, which is fluttering so gracefully from one flower to another.

But the little dog suddenly finds himself at a fence, which forces him to give up the chase. He soon forgets all about it though, for on the other side of the fence, a flock of sheep is grazing. When they hear Max barking, they raise their timid heads in fear and the flock runs away.

11 The countryside wake-up call

"The countryside is lovely," thinks Max, "but what a lot of noise, especially in the morning!" In the city, the basset is used to lying in his basket, lulled to sleep by the usual noises of the house. Of course, he sometimes jumps when a door bangs or there is a sudden sound from outside in the street.

Here, on the other hand, the early morning is another matter entirely! The rooster makes sure of that by crowing at the top of his voice from the first light of dawn. There is no way that it is possible to get back to sleep with a racket like that going on!

12 Fun in the rain!

Since it is impossible to laze around in his basket in the morning, Max decides that he might as well go out into the open air right away, especially as the piercing cry of the rooster has awakened all the other birds, and they are now chirping and twittering and trilling all over the place!

After a while, Skip starts up as well, and barks so insistently and stubbornly that soon all the other dogs on the neighboring farms join in with just as much enthusiasm!

Max, who is lucky enough to sleep in the house, has started whining and howling as well, until someone opens the door to let him out into the garden to join everyone else.

But this morning it is raining; a light rain which wets the ground, the fields, the leaves on the bushes, and the trees.

Max meets up with Skip, who is soaked already, and together the basset and the fox-terrier trot along a path down which the water is gushing. Then the two dogs dive happily into the warm mud, rolling in it playfully, and get absolutely filthy. When Max gets home he is unrecognizable. "Where did you get into such a mess?" Catherine asks him, but she gets no answer. Max just shakes himself and wags his tail.

13 The view from outside

Sitting down beside the wire fence of the henhouse, Max the basset hound, looks on with interest as Flora, the farmer's wife, gathers up the day's eggs. All around the hens scratch and peck at the ground, clucking and wobbling their little red crests from side to side.

Flora puts her hand into one nest, then another one, and pulls out first two, then three white eggs. Max would like to go inside the chicken coop... but on her way out, Flora bolts the door — as usual!

14 A visit to the rabbit hutch

Catherine and her friend Beatrix go with Flora to the rabbit hutch, the cage where the rabbits are kept.

"It can't be very nice to be kept in a cage all the time," observes Catherine.

"If it wasn't like that they would soon become wild rabbits and they would cause a lot of damage, because they reproduce very quickly," replies Flora.

"I would still rather be a wild rabbit," says Catherine stubbornly, but Flora is not listening to her anymore. She is too busy feeding her rabbits with dry bread and carrots.

"My goodness, what strong teeth they have!" exclaims Catherine. "I could never break a crust like that with just one bite!"

In the next cage there is a surprise. The big, grey rabbit has given birth to five baby rabbits with round faces and pointed ears.

"I would really like to pat them," whispers Catherine.

"Definitely not!" says Flora, "If you did, you would leave the smell of your hand on them. After that, the mother would be worried by the smell and would stop feeding them and looking after them."

15 An intruder in the henhouse

One afternoon, a neighbor came to visit Flora while she was still busy in the henhouse. When she had finished her work, Flora was so busy chatting with her friend that she closed the door, but forgot to bolt it.

Hens are very sensible, and they wouldn't dream of leaving the henhouse, but Max, who is very nosy, immediately took the chance of getting inside.

As soon as Flora had disappeared around the hedge, he pushed open the forbidden door, and went into the chicken coop. He caused chaos. The hens started running around in every direction, desperately beating their wings, squawking with fear. Naturally, the rooster cried louder than any of them. Max was having a great time, barking like mad, as he chased the unfortunate birds all over the place.

All the noise brought Flora and Mike, her husband, rushing out of the farmhouse armed with a broom and a stick. After a few moments, they chased the intruder out of the henhouse.

"You deserve a good slap on those long ears of yours, you naughty dog!" exclaimed Flora, waving the broom at Max.

16 The woodchucks wake up

Up on the mountainside, in the den dug out of the earth, at the foot of the rocks, there is a lot of activity. After the long winter sleep, it is time for the marmots to venture out.

As soon as the father woodchuck has moved the stone which blocks the entrance, he puts his nose out to test the temperature. He is blinded for a short while by the bright, spring light. The warmth of the air is a pleasure after the long winter and the smell of the flowers makes him light-headed.

"It's time to come out," he calls. "It's lovely outside! You can all come out."

17 Breakfast on the grass

During the months spent hibernating in their dens under the ground, the woodchucks have become very thin. Just think, at the beginning of the winter, they weighed about thirteen pounds but, when they wake up in the spring, they are only half that weight. So the poor, little woodchucks are very weak and hungry. They need to eat lots of nourishing and tasty food very quickly to make them strong again.

The woodchucks do not find this a hard task! They waste no time in getting to work. From now on, their long days will be spent as much as possible out in the open. The meadows have a lovely fragrance and are covered in flowers! The woodchucks take deep breaths of fresh air, and that stimulates their appetites. "I'm so hungry, so hungry!" mutters a little one, attacking a tuft of tender grass. "We're so hungry too!" echo her two little brothers, filling their mouths with pink, round clover flowers.

Meanwhile, the parents have finished their meal and are lying back in the warm grass. But they do not rest for very long, and soon start worrying about their defenseless young. Alert and watchful, they sniff the pure mountain air, fully aware of everything that is going on around them.

"Take care not to go too far away," the mother warns her three young pups. "An eagle or a crow could fly down suddenly and grab you in its sharp claws!"

Fearful, the little woodchucks stop their meal.

"Keep eating. Don't worry. Your father will keep his eyes open and watch," their mother comforts them. Reassured, the three youngsters continue their breakfast on the grass in peace.

18 Spring can be hard work

Now that the woodchucks have got their strength back, they have to devote all their energy to the home. They have to do their spring cleaning.

"The bedding has to be completely replaced," announces mother wood-chuck. "We have to take out all the old straw and replace it with fresh new grass. Come on, there's enough work for everyone."

The three young woodchucks would rather play in the meadows, but they do their best to lend a hand as well.

19 The woodchucks are on guard

Right in the middle of the flowery slope, there is a big, grey, moss-covered rock. Long, long ago, it fell off the mountain which towers over the meadow. Now the rock makes an excellent look-out point, and the woodchucks climb on to the top of it and use it as a guard post.

Standing upright, one beside the other, perfectly still, they watch tirelessly all around them. Nothing escapes their careful, penetrating eyes: not the eagle flying high in the sky, nor the dangerous crow, nor the fox which almost always appears suddenly and without warning.

As soon as the watchful sentries spy any danger, they at once let out high-pitched whistles, which pierce the air all around and tell the other wood-chucks: "Watch out, there's danger!"

Then all the woodchucks in the area, who were busy playing, or jumping, or eating, or sleeping in the sun, rush back into their dens. In a blink of an eye they have all disappeared, almost as if they had been swallowed up by the ground.

Thanks to the early warning given by the sentries, they are all safe and sound.

20 The hillside acrobats

Anna has gone hiking again with her cousin, Mary. While they are resting after their long climb, half-hidden by a rock, they see an extraordinary sight.

On the slope in front of them, a host of little woodchucks has suddenly appeared, and is putting on a show. Playfully they pretend to fight each other. They leap like acrobats, roll over and over, and chase each other madly. Then there is a sudden sharp whistle, and they disappear again as if by magic.

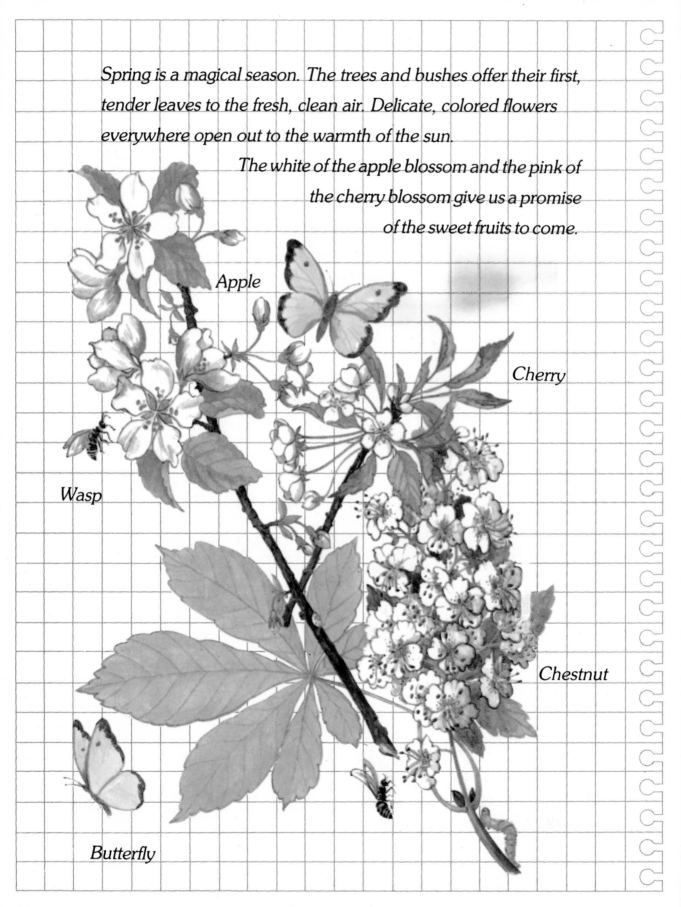

Spring is a magical season. The trees and bushes offer their first, tender leaves to the fresh, clean air. Delicate, colored flowers everywhere open out to the warmth of the sun.

The white of the apple blossom and the pink of the cherry blossom give us a promise of the sweet fruits to come.

Apple

Cherry

Wasp

Chestnut

Butterfly

Eager, little children search the woods for the strawberry and raspberry flowers. They will try to remember the places where they see them, so that they can come back and pick the fruit in the summer.

Raspberries

Redcurrants

Strawberries

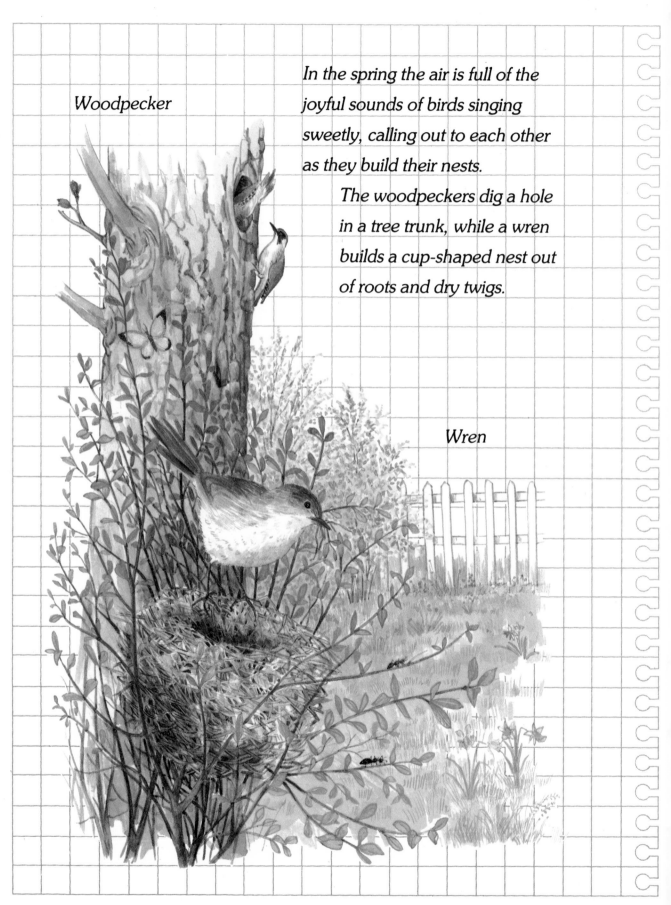

Woodpecker

In the spring the air is full of the joyful sounds of birds singing sweetly, calling out to each other as they build their nests.

The woodpeckers dig a hole in a tree trunk, while a wren builds a cup-shaped nest out of roots and dry twigs.

Wren

The crow makes its nest out of twigs at the top of a poplar tree. The robin redbreast weaves a basket of moss in a tree.

Crow

Robin redbreast

43

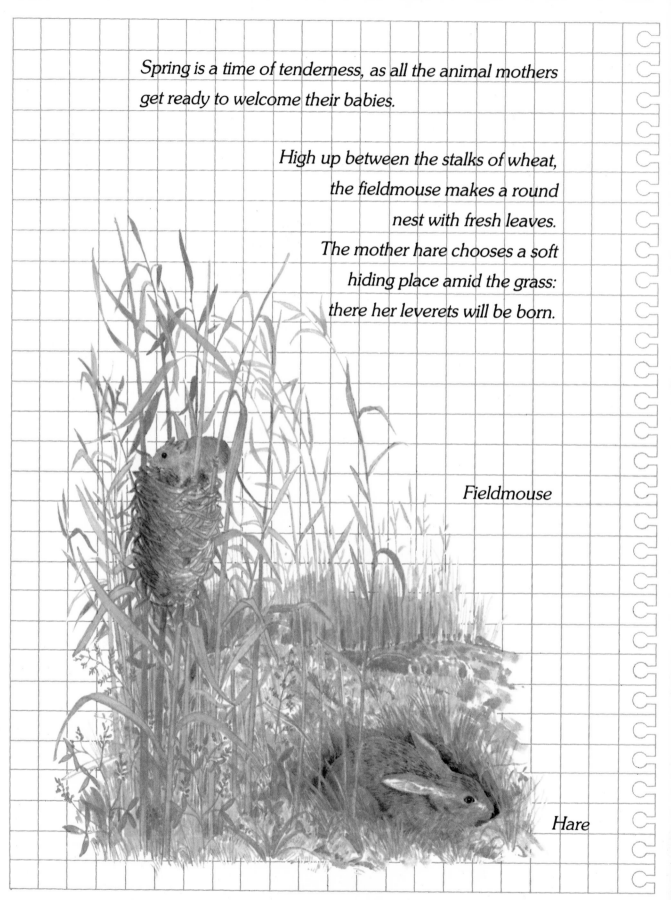

Spring is a time of tenderness, as all the animal mothers get ready to welcome their babies.

High up between the stalks of wheat,
the fieldmouse makes a round
nest with fresh leaves.
The mother hare chooses a soft
hiding place amid the grass:
there her leverets will be born.

Fieldmouse

Hare

The squirrels repair a nest, abandoned by crows, and turn it into a comfortable home.
The deer prepares a bed of grass and dried leaves: it will be the cradle for her fawn.

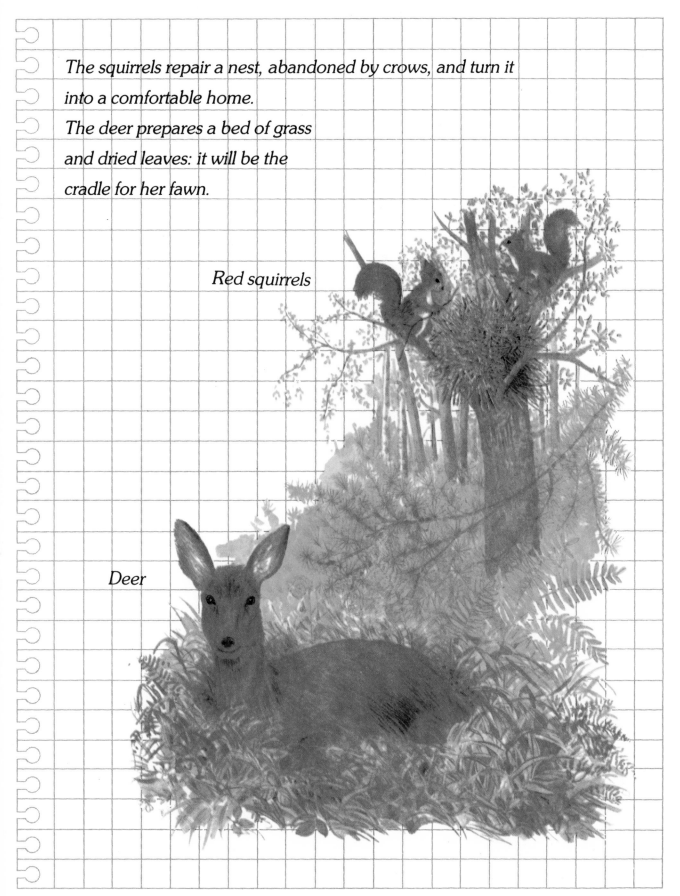

Red squirrels

Deer

The radiant, spring flowers seem to bring a smile to the gardens. They are filled with sweet-smelling hyacinths, splendid tulips, delicate narcissi and bright jonquils.

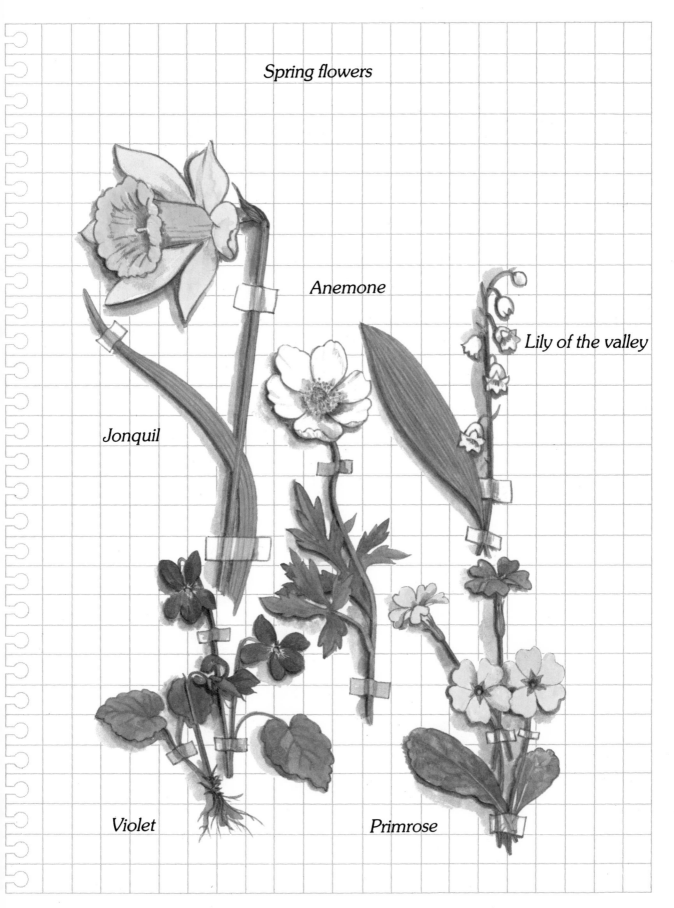

Spring flowers

Jonquil

Anemone

Lily of the valley

Violet

Primrose

Contents

Summer

The great journey

49

The time has come for the flock to say farewell to the warmth of the stable and start moving towards the mountain grazing slopes. Up there, since the winter thaw, the meadows have become covered with tender grass, which will be a source of food for goats and sheep during the summer months.

The air is fresh and pure. The little bells hanging from the animals' necks tinkle with every step they take, and the gentle ringing spreads all around, together with the sounds of the bleating which accompany the slow, calm progress of the flock.

The long parade of sheep and pretty, little lambs, of rams, goats and kids, moves noisily along the country road.

People come out of their houses to watch the summer exodus. Excited children shout and urge the animals on. "Move along, Snowy! Have a good trip, Greybeard!" Sometimes they will pat a sheep which has been left behind, but it soon escapes them and hurries after the others, with nervous bounds.

At the head of the flock is Giles the shepherd, walking at a slow, measured pace, leaning on his long, walking stick. By his side, is the brown donkey that everyone calls Stock-pot, because it carries a large basket, full of provisions for the trip.

At the rear of the procession is Ben, the sheepdog. With his fur all ruffled, running and barking all the time, he seems almost over-excited. But he really is a first class guard dog. Nothing escapes his watchful eye: not the careless goat which wanders off on a side path: nor the lazy ram which would rather stay behind and lie down behind a raspberry bush: nor the little lamb which can't manage to keep up with the flock.

Ben is not afraid of the thunderstorm looming on the horizon, nor the rain shower which is about to fall on the flock. He doesn't fear the night, which comes suddenly, nor the wind which springs up and ruffles the long fleeces of the sheep, which are hiding behind rocks to get away from the rain. The faithful sheepdog is really irreplaceable, and Giles would not know how to get along without him.

The flock passes through a village, and begins climbing a steep path which zig-zags up the mountainside. As they pass, the flock's hooves raise a cloud of dust, which settles again on the path as the animals move on. The great summer journey is under way!

The first night, the flock stops on the edge of a walnut grove, but as soon as

day breaks, they move again, climbing over increasingly steep and rough ground.

As usual, Ben runs from one end of the flock to the other. He notices at once that a kid, a young goat, is having trouble keeping up: its thin little legs keep catching on the stones of the path. Every so often, the kid stops and lets out a sorrowful bleat! The sheepdog runs up and barks madly at Giles, telling him that something is wrong with the flock.

"Ah, it's Snowflake who can't keep up," says Giles, after following the dog back to the struggling kid. "That means we'll have to give you a bit of help," he says, lifting up the inexperienced traveler. It is the first time that the kid is going to the high pastures. Since it was only born in the spring, the journey is too tiring for it. So Giles puts it in one of Stock-pot's baskets, and the exhausted little goat bleats its thanks to him.

After climbing for three days, they reach the splendid mountain meadows, the grazing lands where the flock will spend the summer months. Everything looks wonderful! On the bright green carpet of fresh grass, thousands of yellow buttercups and dark blue flowers brighten the tasty, sweet-smelling grazing ground.

A light breeze spreads delicate fragrances all around. The snow, that still covers the surrounding mountain peaks, keeps the air cool, in spite of the bright sun.

At this altitude, with pure air and a healthy diet, even delicate little Snowflake grows more robust and independent every day. She is no longer recognizable as the timid, little kid, who was always ready to hide behind her mother. Suddenly she has become a real mountaineer. Every day she sets out to explore the surroundings. Fearless, she clambers over rocks, even the steepest ones which stand out on the edge of the meadow. She drinks from the racing stream, which could carry her down the mountain; and then she moves away from the flock to make new discoveries.

Snowflake becomes so daring that one day she slips on the edge of a crevasse! Fortunately, she is caught by a large rhododendron, but she spends a whole night there, hanging on the edge of a steep drop. Ben finds her the next morning, still in the same position, and his barking brings Giles running. The kid is starving and exhausted again, but safe and sound, ready for another adventure! The summer has just begun!

21 A lovely summer morning

The sun rises earlier day by day, because summer days are longer than winter ones. The sky becomes bright at five o'clock in the morning. A distant glow appears on the horizon, so weak that the night still seems to be winning, but gradually the sky brightens into daylight.

The pigeons move on the rooftops and greet the new day in their own way, cooing quietly and endlessly. Over and over again, they seem to be repeating: "Long live the sun! Long live the sun!"

22 Why Michael is late for school

When Michael arrives at school, the big, round, playground clock is definitely showing he is a quarter of an hour late. Michael slinks into the classroom, trying to make himself as inconspicuous as possible, but of course the teacher spots him, and in a severe voice she asks: "Why are you late?"

"It was all the birds' fault," Michael replies. The teacher looks at him in surprise. Michael is an imaginative child, and she is a patient and very understanding teacher... but everything has a limit! Better not ask for further explanations, she thinks, but a word of warning is needed. So she says: "Michael, you mustn't answer with the first thing that comes into your head!"

Michael is upset because he was telling the truth! Since the city has been going through a hot spell of weather, the gardeners in the park water the plants every morning. Today, they had filled a big tub with water. And Michael watched a flock of little birds fly down from a chestnut tree to play in the water, splashing about madly.

That is why he was late for school: it was the birds' fault, the summer's fault.

23 Summer evening on the rooftops

On summer evenings, everyone feels like staying outdoors. Nobody wants to go to sleep; least of all the cats on the rooftops. A cat with a sense of independence likes to clamber up there and go for long, risky walks.

Without any fear of heights, a cat can move with agility from one roof to another, winding its way between the chimney stacks. It will make a short leap now and then, stopping on the edge of a fall. Then it will meow out a passionate serenade into the silence of the night!

24 The seven, large, peaceful carp

We are seven, large, peaceful carp, set in our ways and fond of peace and quiet. We are perfectly content to rest, and spend whole days on the warm, muddy bottom of our large pond. And the fountain, which rises out of a jet in the middle of the pond and falls back as rain, doesn't bother us at all.

Our way of life doesn't bore us. We spend hours contemplating the multi-colored reflections of light on the surface of the water above us. When it rains, a multitude of tiny drops blur its transparency. From time to time, we have to gather our energy and rise to the surface for a breath of fresh air, but apart from this, we lead a very restful life.

Unfortunately, as soon as the summer comes, we have to say goodbye to peace and quiet. Our pond no longer belongs to us. It is invaded by rough, noisy children, who come to sail their boats on it.

Then the water is filled with a whole fleet of boats which the children move with long, bamboo poles; and we have to watch out all the time for these long shapes, passing backwards and forwards overhead.

From time to time, there are collisions, which cause such a splashing on the surface that we become very alarmed. Things become even worse when one of the boats gets trapped in the whirlpools created by the fountain. Rescue operations get under way at once, and you can imagine the panic which occurs down here among us poor carp!

We try to take shelter around the edges of the pond, and there we wait till the worst is past. That is why we, the seven big carp in this pond, do not like fine, summer days at all!

25 To the last ray of light

During the summer, the sun rises very early. Not content with shining for so many hours of the day, it doesn't seem to want to set. The longer period of daylight induces children, and little birds, to put off going to sleep. And while the children use every possible excuse for delaying their bedtime, the little birds, among the leaves of the trees, don't give up either, and continue their incessant chirping.

Even the canary in its cage wants to continue its melodious singing until the last ray of light has passed.

26 Goodbye, parrot friends

It is the last day of school. Everyone is happy. For the whole summer there will be no more rigid rules... but only freedom, games, and fun!

But it is a little sad to say goodbye to the teacher. Luckily, the children will see her again when they return to school. It is also sad to leave the care-taker's two little parrots. The children talked to them every day before going into class.

"Goodbye, parrots, don't talk too much!" call the children, as they leave.

27 A journey for a goldfish

Just the same as every year, Matthew is going to spend a few weeks at his grandparent's house in the country.

The thought of going back to their kitchen, with its huge fireplace, the garden that he knows so well, his cousins and all his other friends, and the life in the open air, all make Matthew very impatient to leave.

He has prepared everything he needs to take, but just as he is about to get into the car, he remembers: "My goldfish! It can't stay here alone. It has to come with us!"

"Certainly," says his mother. "But how can we carry it?" A short family conference is held and they consider various solutions. Eventually, they make a decision; the fish will travel in its usual bowl, avoiding a risky passage from one container to another. The bowl is wrapped up in a plastic bag and placed on a tray with raised edges.

Throughout the whole trip, Matthew keeps the little swimming pool on his knees. In spite of the continual jolting in the car, the movement inside the bowl doesn't exceed the danger level. The little goldfish has a safe journey.

28 Pudding goes on vacation

There is some news for Pudding. He is also going on a trip. He is going with Clare to visit her cousin Barbara.

For the journey, Pudding will be put in a special basket: a wicker basket with lots of openings in its sides so that he can see what is going on outside.

Once in the basket, Pudding finds that it is not too uncomfortable, but he still can't wait to get out as soon as he can. And just to make· this clear to everyone, he doesn't stop meowing for the whole journey!

29 Max, the perfect traveler

Max is used to traveling, even by train. He climbs into the car without any problems. He calmly follows his little mistress along the corridor and, once inside the compartment, he sits down at her feet. When a new passenger enters, Max doesn't blink an eye.

In fact, he would be a perfect traveler if it wasn't for the ticket collector. As soon as he sees the ticket collector, Max gets excited and barks like a mad dog at the poor man. Unfortunately, the little basset hound doesn't like uniforms!

30 Coralbeak gets out of the cage

Another family is leaving for vacation. This time it is Marianne and her little sister Elizabeth. Destination: the seaside.

It was impossible to persuade the two girls to leave home at least some of their favorite things, considering that there were also the two birds to be transported in their cage along with all the rest. So the excess baggage is put on the back seat of the car, the one the two girls are sitting on.

The trip turns out to be longer than expected and Marianne, the more restless of the two, can think of nothing better to do than to open the birds' cage. She lifts up the little gate, and one of the two little birds inside immediately flies out.

Marianne yells: "Coralbeak has flown out of the cage!" The car windows are quickly shut and they pull off the road and stop. A comical hunt then ensues to try and capture the little bird. They all take turns at trying to grab it, but it is not easy. The little bird is incredibly quick and it darts around in an unpredictable manner. Just when it looks like it is about to be caught, it swerves to the side and escapes. All the luggage piled up on the seats provides it with unusual hiding places. Then it flies under the straw hats, which get in the way of the children's attempts to capture the fugitive.

After a good quarter of an hour, Elizabeth manages to grab the bird. She then takes a careful hold of it and gently puts it back in the cage. Marianne, who was sure she had lost her beloved Coralbeak for good, is very happy. Her carelessness will teach her a lesson. It is better to play with her dolls in the car!

1 How tiring to be a sea gull

Running along the pier, Angela thinks: "Wouldn't it be nice to change into a sea gull!"

Why? Because, first of all, it is a very beautiful bird. Its beak and feet are bright red. It has large, pale grey wings, ending in an elegant fringe of black feathers, and it has a tuft on its head of soft, chocolate-colored feathers, which give it a noble look.

What is more, sea gulls have the good luck to live at the sea; they are marine birds. They enjoy the coast and the rocks, where they like to build their nests. Then they go flying across the waves, as they splash and swirl into thousands of different shapes.

One other sure thing about them is they certainly do not have a melodious voice! On the contrary, they cannot sing and they utter only strange, harsh, shrill calls. At times, it seems that the sea gulls are laughing, or making fun of someone, and at other times it seems that they are crying and calling for help.

Most of all, Angela likes the way they live. It must be wonderful to be always moving between the sky and the sea. They take off suddenly and, with powerful beats of their wings, they take advantage of the wind, flying in wide circles, crossing each other's paths, chasing each other, and then calling out and flying even higher.

Just now, the sea gulls have all landed in a line along the pier, and they are walking along as if they were marching in a parade. They stretch out their legs, open their wings, and move their heads backwards and forwards in a very comical manner.

But then they take off again, to welcome the boat coming into port. They fly all around its masts and their cries become louder than ever.

Angela snaps out of her daydream and exclaims: "Ah, well, but it must be very tiring to be a sea gull!"

2 The sea gull and the crab

A sea gull flies silently along the shore: sometimes even sea gulls don't cry out, especially when they are alone. It suddenly spies a large crab moving along in its own peculiar way.

"Where has that crab come from?" the sea gull wonders. "There are no hiding places for it on the beach."

But, in fact, there are: the sand is the best hiding place of all. It seems smooth and deserted, but then, suddenly, out will come a crab to stretch its legs!

3 The shrimp sounds the alarm

It was the smallest, thinnest, little shrimp, which first sounded the alarm. The shrimp was swimming around in the warm water of one of those pools that the sea leaves behind when it withdraws during the low tide. Suddenly it found itself in the webbing of a net.

With very quick reflexes, the shrimp beat its tail, hurried backwards, and swam to safety with the rest of its companions. They all realized what that horrible net meant: the children had arrived for their vacations!

4 Plants in the sea

"If you walk along the shoreline," says Aunt Sophia to Marianne, "it's like being in a garden, but very different garden from normal ones, though it is just as rich in surprises. For example, after the tide goes out you can find plants on the sand."

"Plants?" asks Marianne.

Sophia answers: "Yes, plants that are found in the sea and in fresh water: they are called algae."

"Look!" shouts Marianne, spying some slippery wet strands on the sand. "It looks like salad."

"Those are the green algae, also called "sea lettuce", because they look like garden lettuce," says her aunt. "But there is not just green algae. There is also brown and red algae. The brown ones are very long, sometimes up to a hundred yards: they are the "sequoias" of the sea. They live in the cold seas and are anchored to the sea bottom. The red algae, on the other hand, grows in warm seas and some of their varieties look like lace. They are among the most beautiful of all marine plants."

Marianne is enchanted with all these discoveries, and she becomes more and more curious about these strange and beautiful plants from the sea.

5 The sea's delicate treasures

When the sea withdraws, it doesn't just leave algae on the beach: it also leaves a large number of shells of all shapes and colors.

Aunt Sophia tells her that these shells are the "homes" of marine mollusks. The little girl studies all the different shapes. There are cones, spirals, and scallop shapes. There are smooth and striped shells, some with soft, delicate colors, and mother-of-pearl reflections. Marianne spends hours and hours collecting these delicate treasures.

6 Caught in the net

The four of them met at midday. What a shame it was in such tragic circumstances! They were prisoners in Alexander's drag net! He is an expert fisherman.

The four prisoners are all fine specimens of fish. There is a sole, which is so flat that it doesn't have eyes on both sides of its head: they are both on one side! Then there is a silvery sardine, with large scales. There is a large streamlined mackerel with an elegant tail and finally there is a St. Peter's fish, which is easy to recognize, both for its sullen look and for the dark spot on its silvery grey sides.

How did they all end up in the net? Simply because the unsuspecting sole was lazing around on the sandy sea bed; the sardine was too busy playing; the speedy mackerel was racing through the water, paying no attention to danger, and the St. Peter's fish was busy complaining about a cold current. All of a sudden, all four of them were dragged into the big net. But the mackerel does not despair. It thrashes about wildly in all directions until it has made a big hole in the net! Then all four captives make their escape.

7 A painful encounter in the sand

A crab is moving in its territory: damp sand dunes shaped by the wind, and peaceful, little pools of salt water. Then there is the algae along the shoreline, and lots of shells scattered all around. Away in the distance, the sea is sighing.

The crab advances, quite fast, using its five pairs of claws: the outermost ones, the largest, look like large pliers. Nothing can resist this mighty weapon. The crab uses these claws mostly for feeding. With them it catches fish, worms and mollusks of every type. Lined with sharp, needle-like points,

nothing could be better than these, for gripping, crushing, and opening!

All those who live on the edge of the sea must be warned. Beware of the crab! The same warning goes for the big toes of those bare feet moving around on the sand. They risk being grabbed by those claws, and that means pain for their unlucky owner!

That is just what happened to Mark that afternoon. He just touched the crab which was hiding in the sand with his foot. A very painful experience!

8 A jellyfish floats by

"I am a jellyfish, an animal which lives in the sea. I have a jelly-like body which is transparent and divided into a concave upper part and a convex lower one, in the center of which is my mouth. The double dome which forms my body has eight grasping tentacles around it."

"I know how to swim in a very simple style: contracting and expanding my double umbrella, sucking in and expelling the water. So I move forward very lightly, as if I was dancing. But be careful of me, because my tentacles can cause irritation!"

9 The sea gull's winter vacation

A sea gull, which has spent the winter months in the city, hiding there from the north winds, is now getting ready to return to the ocean. You see, sea gulls don't always live by the sea. When it becomes too cold in the north, some prefer to spend a few months further south, in a city on a river.

"How do they find the way?" some might ask. "Why don't they get lost?" Because, as with all migrating birds, there is no risk of this with sea gulls. From the river's mouth, they travel up the river, resting in the countryside, where they can feed on insects and worms.

So, step by step, they reach the city they have chosen and there they stay throughout the cold months. When city people see the sea gulls coming, they know that the winter is not far away.

But now that the summer has returned, the white sea gull feels nostalgic for the great, ocean spaces, the salty air of the sea, the beaches and the rock faces. And it is on the sea cliffs that the gulls make their nests, seeking the females who are ready for mating.

10 Time for the cuttlefish to move

Long, straight and thin, white or grey in color, the cuttlefish spends hours in the water. When the sea withdraws at low tide, however, the cuttlefish does not follow but buries itself in the sand. It will come out again when the sea returns to cover it.

When a cuttlefish is resting, well protected in its hole, it will feel that the sea water is beginning to cover it again. "It's time to get swimming again," it thinks. "The siesta is over." And then this marine shellfish allows itself to be gently carried away by the water.

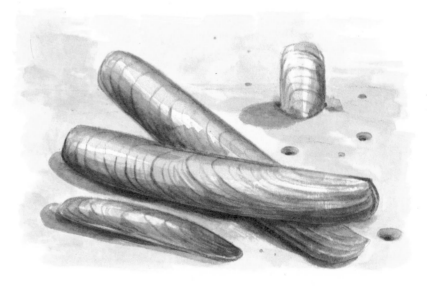

11 The crab's crooked walk

"What a strange way of walking," says a mussel, watching a thick-shelled crab clumsily moving on its daily hunting expedition.

"It's not so strange," adds another mussel. "Yes, the crab has a crooked walk, but that's just how it is. What's wrong with that? Crabs don't know how to walk straight, but still they go everywhere. Look at us, my dear, we're always stuck in the same place. I wish we could get around like our neighbor over there!"

12 The busy, little water fleas

Marianne has become bored staying in one place and playing on the sand. She is also feeling burned by the sun, which means she will have to wear a light dress on the beach for a few days.

Today, she has decided to go and gather shells: it's much more fun, and you can discover lots of new things. So she heads off towards the sand that has been left wet by the sea, and is still all shiny in the sunlight. She comes across lots of algae and shells, half-buried in the sand.

They are all there for the taking! Marianne bends over a long piece of algae, then immediately draws back, horrified, finding a thick cloud of little animals jumping all over it.

"How horrible!" She hurries back to the dry sand. Then her mother persuades her to go back with her, to see just what these jumping animals are.

"They are water fleas," she explains. "They are very busy, little workers and they like to keep a clean house. They look as if they are jumping for no reason, but they are keeping the sand clean, eating all the dead organisms. Even if there are an awful lot of them, they are still always busy!"

13 The enchanted, underwater forest

The algae anchored to the sea bed forms a silent, underwater forest. At times they are moved by the gentle current, just like a breeze, and at times they wave about in the raging currents caused by the sudden storms on the sea.

It is a forest with great variety, dotted with bush-like outgrowths with beautiful, long, waving tendrils: an underwater forest enriched with great, sea anemones and inhabited by a multitude of colorful fish. A real, enchanted forest.

14 The jellyfish loves to eat

The jellyfish is really a very graceful animal, with its wavy umbrellas fringed by tentacles. And it is also very graceful when it swims, the twin domes of its body pulsing rhythmically.

The jellyfish also loves good food: it is not by chance that its mouth is placed right in the middle of its body, in the center of its lower umbrella!

The jellyfish's favorite meal consists of shrimps and other crustaceans: and it just loves plankton.

Plankton? What is that?

Well, plankton comes from the Greek word for wandering, and, in fact, plankton wanders around the sea. It is extraordinarily nourishing: a sort of highly concentrated soup, rich in nutritious substances, made up of microscopic animal organisms, like mollusks, and plants, like algae.

Not only jellyfish live on plankton, but also lots of other marine animals, like the whales, the biggest plankton eaters of all.

Really plankton is a wandering food source, which is carried along by sea currents. A real magic potion!

15 No vacancy on the rock

Not one space has remained empty on the half-submerged rock. All the rooms are taken from the cellar to the roof!

To start with, the cellar has been occupied by a crab. Individual, independent, it comes and goes of its own free will, and it is also really fixed in its ways, so much so that you could set your clock by it.

On the first floor, live two fish: they also come and go at will, but at the strangest times. On their balcony they have grown a curtain of algae which acts as a screen to protect them from prying eyes.

On the second and third floors, live two very large families of mussels, and they make a lot of noise and never go anywhere!

On the third floor, the limpets also live. They are very kind and well-mannered, and they wear a dome-shaped mantle, which means they never leave their house.

On the top floor, the penthouse apartment with a terrace and swimming pool, are the shrimps, who lead a very calm life.

And finally on the roof, occasionally, two sea gulls will visit for a while, then fly off again.

16 Three unusual sea creatures

There are three inhabitants of the sea, the scorpion fish, the moray eel and the octopus, which look more like creatures of the imagination than ones which really exist.

Of the three, the scorpion fish, which is also called the "sea scorpion", is notorious for its ugliness. This is not surprising, because its big, reddish head, armored with hard bony plates, is covered with poisonous needles. It has large, deep furrows which give it a truly unpleasant appearance. As if that wasn't enough, its poisonous barbs can be made to stick out from the rest of its body.

The moray eel is not so ugly, but it is long and thin, with a skin which is mottled in lively, bright colors. It is a very ferocious creature, with razor sharp teeth ending in sharp hooks. The moray eel attacks and devours its prey by dashing out of the cracks in the rocks where it lies in hiding.

The third creature, the octopus, is not a fish but a large mollusk. It is not aggressive, but it is renowned for the extraordinary strength of its tentacles. Its head can look scary, as the octopus has two protruding eyes, surrounded by waving tentacles, which are covered with many grippers on the undersides!

17 The silvery, little mullets

Seven small mullets are wandering lazily about, heedless of what goes on around them, going nowhere in particular. Here and there, they stop for a while above a white sandbank.

The mullet's large head, a bit flat with a short, rounded face, gives this peaceful fish a naive, gentle look. As soon as they see the surface of the sea shining up above, with short beats of their tail they swim swiftly up to the surface and launch themselves into the air, almost as if they had been made deliriously happy!

The silvery scales of these mullets shine in the rays of the sun when they leap out of the water. Then they disappear immediately, as if they had never been there. But the fun goes on and, at regular intervals, they repeat their joyful leaps. The little mullets really enjoy this game, but all the activity gives them an appetite: and so they all dive down to the bottom, to find some tasty algae to eat.

18 The dance of the scallops

Some young sardines met some scallops for the first time. The sardines took a thorough look at these mollusks, with their elegant double shells, while they were resting on the sand. All of a sudden, the shells moved away, towards the forest of algae.

As they move, it is almost as if they are dancing a lively polka: it is just their way of moving. They open their valves and suck in a little water, then they push it out, snapping their shells shut. It is this action that propels them forward.

19 How an octopus defends itself

After finishing its meal of cockles and crabs, the octopus sets off for home, sliding over the sea bed by using its strong tentacles.

For its home, it has chosen a natural cave opening in the rocks, and as soon as it reaches it, the octopus disappears inside. A few minutes later, however, it appears again out of its protected hiding place, and swims in its own, very unusual fashion.

By an ingenious, very simple system, an octopus swells its large central sack with water, which it then empties out all at once. This forcibly expelled water enables the big mollusk to move forward in a series of leaps.

If an octopus has to escape from a predator while it is outside its cave, it can use one of two defenses. When it is being chased, it can suddenly change color, which can confuse the predator. Or it can spray out a black liquid, like ink, creating an impenetrable cloud which allows it to slip away from its enemy.

The strange-looking octopus has many ways of defending itself and getting out of trouble.

20 The voracious starfish

"Run, Aunt Sophia, hurry!" shouts Marianne excitedly. "I've found a starfish and it's all red!"

"Isn't it beautiful?" says her aunt: "It's still moving... put it on the wet sand and the sea will take it away again."

"It is very pretty, like the pattern on my sun dress," says Marianne, putting it down reluctantly.

"Starfish are very elegant... and also very voracious," explains her aunt. "This pretty, little creature is quite capable of devouring a whole assortment of mollusks and think nothing of it!"

21 The sea's regular movements

Do you know what tides are? They are the regular movements which the sea makes twice a day. First of all, bit by bit, it withdraws down the beach... and then it will climb back up as far as the dry top of the beach. This regular movement is caused by the moon, which periodically attracts and releases the water in the sea. If you want to know more about this, you should ask your parents or your teacher for a full explanation.

On the other hand, if you just want to know how Marianne discovered tides, here is the story. On the same day that she arrived at the sea for her vacation, Marianne went down to the beach with her Aunt Sophia and together they built a sand castle, on the best part of the beach for building castles, where the sand remains damp.

A few hours later, they had created a real masterpiece: a mighty fortress, with four strong towers and battlements, strengthened by large and small seashells, a main gate in the middle, all surrounded by a deep moat.

Marianne clapped her hands with joy. "Well done, well done, Aunt Sophia!" The little girl had never seen such a beautiful castle! She stood proudly by it, surrounded by all the other children on the beach who had come to admire the magnificent building.

Then a sudden noise caused her to turn her head. And she saw that the sea was coming very fast towards her, faster and faster it seemed, so that the water was already swirling around her feet.

"My castle," she screamed. "Be careful! The sea will destroy my castle!" But the sea wasn't listening, and it still advanced. Aunt Sophia had to take Marianne by the hand and drag her onto the dry part of the beach, while the castle was swiftly surrounded by water, and then began to crumble bit by bit, until it was all swallowed up by the tide.

22 The smallest crabs

Do you know what the smallest crab measures? Half an inch; more or less the same size as a grain of rice. And yet, even though it is so small it is nonetheless a proper crab, with five pairs of legs and a delicate, soft body armor.

The smallest crab has a very difficult name that is hard to remember. The family is called Pinnotheridae, or the pear crabs. And do you know where they live? Inside mollusks, such as mussels. A very large home for such a small crab!

23 The greedy herring gulls

The herring gull must be one of the greediest of all birds. It is forever hungry, and its favorite food is shellfish. Now, as we all know, shellfish are delicious to eat, but how does the herring gull get through their protective shells?

The gull uses a simple, very obvious method to break the shells. It picks up the shellfish in its beak, then takes off and flies to a certain height. When it is over rocks, it drops the shellfish onto them, breaking the shell open, so that the bird can eat without difficulty.

24 Herring gulls and fish

After it has dropped the shellfish onto the rocks, the herring gull has to dive down very quickly and snatch its meal. If it is too slow, some other herring gull will swoop down and steal its snack!

If the shell turns out to be very hard, the herring gull repeats the operation, but this time will try to smash the shell against bigger rocks, until finally it succeeds.

A bird as greedy as the herring gull is never going to be satisfied with just shellfish. It is also very fond of fish; but fortunately for the fish, it is not very good at fishing. In fact, it hardly knows how to fish at all! So it has to make do with dead fish washed up on the shore and left behind by the tides. The herring gull devours all these with enthusiasm, and, without knowing it, by cleaning the whole beach, it makes itself very useful.

25 Herring gulls, worms, and old fruit

After its fine meal of shellfish and fish, the gull now feels like some meat! So it leaves the coast behind and flies off inland, towards the countryside where, thanks to its very keen eyesight, it has no difficulty in spotting large worms in the fields.

It is still not satisfied, so it then flies back towards the sea, pausing at the mouth of the harbor. Here it chooses from the debris of vegetables and fruit peelings floating on the water.

Flying from one place to another, the herring gull never stops eating!

26 The aerial acrobats

Born during the full moon, in the safety of Jenny's mailbox, the little larks have now grown up. They have even left the garden, but they haven't gone very far away! They have settled just beyond the garden wall, amid the thick branches of the beautiful acacia tree.

From time to time, they indulge in acrobatic competitions. Their favorite trick is a double loop-the-loop, which causes great excitement among the other little birds in the neighborhood: one, two, three, hop, hop, hop!

27 The enchanted wood

The hot days of high summer are suffocating. Under the burning rays of the midday sun, the earth cracks into great clods, the grass shrivels up and the leaves hang limp on the trees.

In the fields and meadows, and even in the woods, all the animals are in search of someplace cool.

At this time of the day, the snail withdraws further and further into its shell and the worm into its long hole. The ants interrupt their constant coming and going to take shelter under some slender blades of grass. The butterflies take a nap in the cool shade of the honeysuckle. The bees suspend their constant buzzing. The hornets sit motionless on the flowers. The birds stop their singing, and tuck their heads under their wings, sitting quietly amid the leaves on the trees.

The country mouse is in the middle of a deep sleep at the bottom of its den, and certainly won't poke its head out until night has fallen. The fieldmice are also hiding from the sun, beneath some ferns. There is a strange stillness, almost as if a fairy has waved her magic wand and put all the inhabitants of the woods to sleep. Maybe it was the Summer Fairy!

28 Five bushy-tailed squirrels

Five, lively, little squirrels jump from branch to branch: do you recognize them? They are the squirrels who were born on the big pine tree two months ago.

Of course, they have changed a lot. Now they are strong, swift and alert, ready to sprint through the trees. Now they also have magnificent red coats.

They move busily among the roots of the big pine tree, one moment racing to the top, and the next descending just as swiftly. In between, they spend time delicately smoothing their thick tails, almost as if they were at the beauty parlor!

29 A row of hedgehogs

On the white, gravel path, four hedgehogs are moving along in short, scurrying bursts. The four prickly, little shapes are all in a row, stopping at the slightest sound: the rustling of a leaf, or the whirring of a moth's wings.

The little family of four trots along the garden path. It is partly a caravan in search of its daily food, and partly an adventurous trip. Slowly they disappear into the thick foliage.

30 The leveret's godmothers

"Did you see it?" asks the blackcap, pointing towards the honeysuckle with its beak.

"Yes, it is very pretty," confirms a blackbird, with its fine black feathers and yellow beak.

"It is also very nice," adds the lark. "I live just opposite, in the beech trees, and I can see it very clearly. It hardly moves, and it makes no noise. It is perfectly happy to watch the leaves swaying in the wind and the bees on the flowers."

"But do they always leave it by itself?" the blackbird asks.

"No," replies the lark, who knows everything. "In the evening, its mother comes to give it milk."

"Thank goodness for that! It looks so defenseless. I would be very sorry to see it abandoned," says the blackbird.

"The owl told me that it was a leveret," announces the blackcap.

"A leveret? Well, then it is a young hare!" exclaims the blackbird.

"Whatever it is, it is very sweet," the lark chirps cheerily. "I am glad that it has come to stay here with us."

"Tweet, tweet, chirp, chirp." The three "godmothers" continue their gossiping around the honeysuckle bush.

31 The little rabbit pays no attention

"Yes, I know!" says the little rabbit, who between one leap and another has landed in a field of clover. He is so busy running, jumping and rolling over that he is not listening to anyone.

And yet it is important for him to listen to what his mother tells him: "Beware of the weasel."

"Yes, yes, don't worry," answers the little rabbit.

Sooner or later, he is going to have to pay attention to his mother, because the rabbit's most dangerous enemy is the weasel.

1 The squirrels' parachutes

It is not just vanity that makes the squirrels constantly groom their tails with their tiny, pointed tongues, and comb them with their little paws. They are cleaning them of all the twigs and pine needles which get caught in them, and the blobs of resin which stick in the thick fur and make the tails heavier.

Nor is it vanity which leads these lovely little creatures to puff up their tails to make them soft and fluffy, and shake them out like feathers! It is actually simple prudence that makes them do it all. For squirrels, a tail is not just a simple ornament, a lovely decoration on their bodies which makes them so pretty and friendly: most of all they use their tails as parachutes!

A tail is a small, but efficient parachute which enables a squirrel to jump out of the top of a fir tree without getting hurt in the process. It allows them to jump freely from branch to branch, and fly away at the first sign of danger.

But if their tail is to work properly as a parachute, it has to be kept clean always and brushed, soft and airy.

2 Nocturnal voices

It is a hot, August night. Clare has left the window wide open, turning off her lamp so that the biting mosquitoes won't be attracted into her room.

She can't seem to get to sleep because of the stifling air, and can only lie there and listen to the soft, nocturnal sounds. Clare has no trouble at all identifying the screech of an owl, the monotonous, incessant croaking of the frogs, who are calling to each other in the pond, the insistent barking of the neighbor's dog, or the soft rustling of the poplar leaves.

She hears the sound of a car moving along the road; and, up above, in the barn, she hears the usual night-time rustling of the mice. Closer at hand, a soft rustling reveals the presence of a moth fluttering around the bedroom.

But, all of a sudden, above all these subdued noises, there arises a melodious sound, the pure, clear song of a bird, with one sweet note succeeding another. It is the smooth, melodious voice of the nightingale; but to Clare it sounds like Prince Charming singing just for her!

3 How to eat properly

The five squirrels which live on the big pine tree are still at work. This time, however, they are not busy cleaning themselves, they are learning how to eat properly, or something like that. They are learning how to chew into a pine cone.

First of all, they have to learn to keep the cone upright in a firm grip between their paws. Then, using their sharp front teeth, they have to learn to nibble through and discard the outer scales. Only in this way will they manage to extract the small, sweet-smelling, tasty pine-seeds.

4 The green flash of a lizard

In the shade of the oleander, the cicada sings noisily. It is singing about the joys of summer, the clear sky, the sun which shines and makes everything bright, the rich fragrance of the flowers and the sweetness of the air.

Johnny, as he is passing by the oleander, covered with its pink flowers, stops for a moment and listens. He wishes he could catch sight of the little, singing cicada, but even with his sharp eyes he is unable to find its hiding place. He even sits down on the dry stone wall, and carefully runs his eyes over the flower-covered plant, leaf by leaf, branch by branch.

Then, suddenly, right beside him, he sees a flash of green. What could it be? Johnny stares, without moving, at a crack in the wall, absolutely silent. He is no longer interested in the cicada!

The little, green creature comes out of the crack again: it is slender, lively, covered in tiny scales, with a small pointed head, and a long, long tail. Johnny has no difficulty in recognizing the lizard.

There is always something enchanting in Nature's treasury! In place of a cicada that can't be seen, Johnny sees a green, flashing lizard!

5 The magician and the watering-can

The August sun acts like a magician. It spreads its mantle of sun-drenched heat over all the flowers in the gardens, warming all of them. It gives health to the apple tree, and strengthens the creeping plants adorning the walls of the old house. It makes the mowed lawn look like a green carpet, dotted with bright flowers in a variety of colors.

But what a thirst the sun causes in all of them. And so, the watering-can gets no rest. It has to work very hard to cool down all the geraniums, petunias, dahlias and zinnias.

6 The ladybug plant-cleaners

Jenny is studying the flowering rose bush, fascinated by the beauty of the sweetly perfumed flowers. Looking at it close up, she also sees lots of ladybugs climbing along the branches, moving about amidst the soft petals. "I know that they are so pretty, but I wonder if the ladybugs damage the roses?" Jenny asks.

"On the contrary," replies her mother. "The ladybugs clean the roses of aphids, those tiny insects which stick onto the leaves, the flowers and the buds, infesting and weakening the whole plant."

7 An orchard of delights

With Pudding the cat in her arms, Clare has come to say hello to Emily. She finds her in the orchard, seated in the shade of a lovely apricot tree. A little further away, Vanilla, Pudding's mother, is sleeping, curled up in the grass of the meadow.

It is hot and the fragrance of the flowers spreads through the air. Some butterflies are flying around in their usual carefree manner.

A light breeze ruffles the leaves of the trees and causes their colorful fruits to wave about.

Clare can see lots of red velvety peaches in the orchard and her mouth starts to water. Then she sees a row of apricot trees, heavily laden with their sweet-smelling, yellow-orange fruits. She also recognizes plum trees, but their fruits are still unripe and do not yet have that violet blue color which shows when they are fully ripe.

"Good morning, Emily," says Clare. "What are you going to do with all the fruit on these trees?"

"Ah, that is a secret," Emily replies, looking mysterious. "It's a sweet secret! But if you are good, I'll tell you about it soon."

8 A dragonfly passes by

A low, buzzing noise makes the air vibrate. Mark, who had been running, stops in his tracks. "That sounds like a glider," he thinks. "Yes, definitely a small glider!" Then he turns towards the tree and spies an unusual insect. It has a small round head, with round eyes sticking out, on a shiny blue, thin, tapering body. Two pairs of transparent wings gleam as it flies in a graceful, gliding fashion.

It is a dragonfly, of course, but to Mark it is nothing less than a miniature glider!

9 Back to the pond

I think that we should go back to the pond to see how the seven little ducklings are doing. Here they are! They are completely unrecognizable! That is not surprising, if you think about all they have eaten for days and days! But not only have they grown; their plumage has changed completely. Now they are totally covered with lovely brown and grey feathers. Now they look very elegant and resemble their mother.

It was during the month of June, when the yellow irises were flowering by the banks of the pond, that their coats underwent this transformation. At the same time, our ducklings changed into young wild ducks.

They also began then to change their behavior. Now the seven young ducks can move around the pond at will, no longer under the watchful eye of their mother. And the inquisitive youngsters take full advantage of this new state of affairs!

They explore the most remote corners of their domain; they dive down deep under the roots of the old willow tree; they wind their way through the aquatic plants and they swim happily between the flowering banks. They stick their beaks in everywhere, splashing and paddling about. From time to time, they even visit relatives who live in the pond, like their cousins, the divers, and they enjoy challenging each other to games of hide and seek among the reeds, and they hold races against the moorhens.

Today, something very important happened: one of them learned how to fly. After repeated attempts with uncoordinated wing beats, the young duck suddenly took off from the pond.

Incredible! His brothers and sisters watch him in admiration and envy. "Don't worry, your turn will come soon," their mother reassures each of them.

10 The mill-stream and the blue diver

Jean is by the stream today, the one which powers the wheel at her aunt's mill.

It is a noisy stream which bubbles along from rock to rock, tumbling through the reeds, frothing under the long branches of the weeping willow, until it rushes over a waterfall and finally races away under the little wooden bridge.

Jean is enjoying watching the little whirlpools of silvery water, when, all of a sudden, a bird as blue as the sky dives into the stream!

11 The fantastic kingfisher

A fantastic bird with shiny, blue feathers races across the surface of the water: it is the kingfisher. As its name suggests, its skill at fishing is legendary.

It has neither a line nor a hook, but it does have a much more effective, efficient tool in its beak, which is strong, large, fast-moving and ideal for fishing.

But this marvelous beak would be useless if the kingfisher didn't know how to use it to perfection, like the craftsman it is. Perched on a willow branch overhanging the water, the bird remains absolutely still. It looks all around, staring for a long time at the river bottom, waiting patiently.

As soon as a fish passes beneath it, the kingfisher dives straight into the stream. It keeps its wings close to its body, grabbing the fish in its long, sharp beak at the first attempt.

After the successful hunt, the kingfisher returns to the surface and takes up the same motionless posture on the willow branch. It is again ready to drop down on another poor fish which will pass by, completely un-aware of the danger poised above.

12 A clean river full of fish

The river flows gently between its flowering banks, under the hanging branches of the willow trees. In the clear, clean water, reflections can be seen of the blue sky, the clouds, the reeds, and the trees which grow along its banks.

But underneath the calmly flowing surface is the rich world of the freshwater fish. Each fish has its own space, where it hides, and its play area; and the habits and preferences of one species are very different from another's.

The trout, for example, love to swim around close to a waterfall, where the water is rough and foamy.

Calm depths are the favorite places for the lazy carp, who will stay motionless for hours beneath the warm sun. The dark-backed perch, on the other hand, are always ready to come up to the surface.

Then there are the mighty bream with their silvery scales, who go on long explorations in groups, and the lively roach who can't keep still for a moment; and the little gudgeon who blend in with the river bed where they like to live. Then there is the rudd with its red eyes and fins, and the golden tench. A clean river can be quite crowded with fish!

13 Seven young ducks in flight

Today all the young ducks from the pond have flown off together. They are now perfectly capable of flying whenever they wish, and it must be a great joy for them to feel the wind flowing over their feathers!

Their new game is to take off and discover new places from the air. The seven young explorers are really reluctant to fly back to their quiet pond.

It is so exciting to be able to fly high in the blue sky, with nothing in their way!

14 The dance of the dragonflies

There are some ballet dancers who don't need special shoes, or ballet costumes, or the music of an orchestra, in order to dance. They are ballet dancers who have no need of stage settings, or lights, or floors to pirouette on. And yet their pirouettes and movements are just as light and graceful as those of any trained dancers.

These extraordinary dancers are the dragonflies. Just look at their costume. Light, transparent wings are attached to a thin, tapered body, finer than any silken garments.

The natural settings in which they dance are without doubt more beautiful than scenes set up on the stage, inside any theater. Just look at the watery environments they use as a background. The surface of the water is adorned with lilies, colored a delicate yellow, pink or white, and lit by the radiant light of the sun hanging low on the horizon.

The dragonflies dance through this lovely, natural setting, accompanied only by the soft rustling of the reeds in the wind, and the musical gurgling of the nearby stream!

15 The kingfishers' nest

Do you know how the kingfishers build their nest? And, do you have any idea where they do it? On an elm tree or a weeping willow, along the banks of the river? No! Kingfishers build their nest at the end of a tunnel. For up to three weeks, the birds work very hard to dig a tunnel into the riverbank, removing stones, roots and clods of earth. The nest is built at the end of this tunnel.

Isn't it strange that this bright blue, flashing bird should welcome its young into the world in the dark?

16 An odd bed for young kingfishers

Another unusual thing about the kingfishers' nest is its lining! I bet you cannot imagine what these splendid, blue-feathered birds choose to line the nests of the young kingfishers who are about to be born?

What would you expect the parent kingfishers to carry down the long tunnel to the nest? Perhaps moss, blades of grass, leaves, feathers? Or twigs, hay stalks, bits of bark, down?

No, you're quite wrong. The kingfishers line their soft nests with small fish bones!

17 The ugly, little kingfishers

Well protected in its hiding place along the banks of the river, a female kingfisher has laid six white eggs, which she is now ready to brood over with amazing patience.

Outside, the sun is shining brightly, the river is flowing peacefully, and the leaves on the trees sway gently. But the female kingfisher has to stay perfectly still in the dark and the silence.

Fortunately, the male kingfisher keeps her company. He brings tasty little fish in his beak and, as a dessert, succulent dragonflies.

Then he helps pass the time by telling her some funny bird stories! From time to time he even sings, and she will also pick up the tune, and then the two sing a harmonious duet!

So, the time passes quickly and eighteen days are soon over. Six tiny, little birds then begin to tap on their shells. However, when they finally appear they are really ugly, with matted feathers that look like needles! All they want is to be fed. As they grow, they start more and more resembling their beautiful parents, with their marvelous, soft plumage, as shiny as silk: the famous blue plumage of the kingfisher.

18 So much good food

The kingfisher is a real expert at finding suitable food for the raising of its young.

It captures fat, green, blue and grey flies: all colors which stimulate their appetites. And it even prepares them by removing the wings, so that the youngsters can swallow them without any difficulty.

Or else it hunts down the dragonflies, which are highly sought after for their delicate flavor, and after taking the wings off them as well, it flies back as fast as it can to feed these tasty morsels to its young.

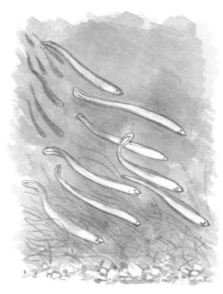

19 The strange story of the eel

Do you know the story of the eel? It is an amazing one. When it is adult, the eel is like a small, black serpent. It lives in tidal waters and rivers, but it is not born there. In fact, the life cycle of the eel is a great adventure.

Eels are born in the huge forest of giant algae in the Sargasso Sea off the southern coast of North America. At first, an eel looks like a transparent fish with a flat, elongated body, measuring only a few inches.

Yet it leaves its safe refuge among the algae and allows itself to be carried along by the warm waters of the Gulf Stream towards the coasts of Europe.

It is an heroic enterprise! These little creatures, which are not yet called eels, are exposed to an incredible variety of dangers, from voracious predator fish to the strong ocean currents. How they ever manage to stay on course is still a complete mystery! But still the little migrants set out to challenge fate.

During their journey, they grow longer and thinner. And then one fine day, when they are in sight of the coastline of Europe, they head towards the mouths of rivers, which they then follow upstream into the heart of the land mass. There, the little eels of the future make their homes, continuing to develop, putting on weight and becoming darker in color.

But their transformation is not yet over. The young eels continue to grow until they become long, fat, shiny adult eels, capable of wriggling across dry land from one body of water to another during the night.

After five years, the eels go back down river, and cross the ocean again as far as the Sargasso Sea, where, at last, they lay their eggs. From these, other tiny eels are born and they in turn repeat the great migration of their parents.

And so, the life cycle repeats itself endlessly.

20 The pair of kingfishers

The pair of kingfishers who fly through the sky in perfect harmony seem almost inseparable!

Now that their young have learned how to fly and fish for themselves, the parent birds are once again free to fly together for long trips over the river, following all their usual pathways. They fly in harmonious and elegant formation, their bodies stretched taut and their wings spread wide, their heads pointing straight forward. These lovely blue birds are so beautiful that anyone watching them can only be filled with joy.

21 The tiny, light fieldmouse

It can be very convenient, sometimes, being small, so very, very, small, and as light as a fieldmouse. It is only because it is so light and small that it is able to remain hidden in the wheat, certain that no one will be able to discover it; or else climb to the very top of a blue cornflower; or hang by its tail from a golden ear of wheat, without bending the stalk!

To be able to carry out acrobatics like this you really must be very small, two inches at the most; and very light, two ounces at the most!

22 A nest full of flowers

There are country creatures which are even smaller than the tiny fieldmouse! It is a riddle of course! They are the newborn babies of a fieldmouse. At birth, they are only one inch long and weigh less than one ounce.

These little, tiny fieldmice are very pretty, with their lively faces, their walnut-colored fur, soft and fleecy, and their tiny, flexible tails.

The female fieldmouse can give birth to litters several times a year, and each time she builds a completely new nest. During the summer, she builds between two ears of wheat. She works very quickly, but very precisely. Her sharp teeth are used to cut the leaves into narrow strips. Then, skilfully using her paws, she binds them and weaves them together into a round, padded basket. But the job is not yet finished: the nest now has to be properly decorated.

Now the mouse goes out and gathers a buttercup petal here and a convolvulus flower there, then a piece of cornflower and a thin slice of poppy, and she places these at the bottom of the nest, where they make up a soft cushion. Now her nest is filled with flowers and their lovely perfume, all ready to welcome her new batch of babies.

23 The flowers amid the wheat

Amid the fully grown wheat in the field, some brightly colored, wild flowers are also growing. They are very pretty but not particularly welcome to the farmers, who don't want any intruders among their golden ears of wheat.

But the insects do not agree with them. Crickets and grasshoppers have great fun playing in these flowers, and they spend long periods lying in the soft petals of the poppies; or else they go for a walk on top of the blue cornflowers, and then take a rest on the yellow cushion of a daisy!

24 The lark as an informer

Inside the wheat field there is a hidden and very diverse world. So perhaps we should ask someone who lives there all about it; the lark, for example, who spends hours and hours among the stalks of wheat.

The lark is a lively, sweet, little bird. It always wakes early and flies off immediately, singing joyful songs. It sings out the extraordinary beauty of the rising sun and the marvels of the birth of a new day. Then it swiftly flies back down and lands in the wheat field.

"Lark, little lark, would you be our informer and tell us what is happening inside that sea of wheat?"

"Lark, little lark, tell us how the mice are getting along." The lark shakes its feathers, grey slightly tinged with brown, and with a sweet chirping replies: "Just now the mice are still very small; they are only three days old! They are moving, round, and round in their little nest, tumbling on the soft petals. Then they drink some milk from their mother and fall contentedly asleep. That's all I can tell you just now!"

And, saying this, the lark flies off.

25 The rumble of thunder

The sun hangs over the countryside like a leaden disc, and an oppressive heat presses down on the fields. In the woods, there is not a breath of wind; the leaves on the trees are perfectly still; even the meadows show no signs of life.

A heavy silence lies over the little valley. It seems as if all the animals have suddenly fallen silent: among the leafy branches the birds have stopped their twittering; even the buzzing of the insects has ceased. As well as keeping silent, the inhabitants of the woods have also gone into hiding. There is no one to be seen! The rabbits have disappeared from the clover fields and the squirrels from the pine trees. Even the deer, which a short while ago were leaping in the clearing, are now nowhere to be seen.

A strange unease has taken hold of all of them: the animals are nervous, worried and jumpy. The sky is growing darker: the metallic steel-grey light makes it seem sinister and threatening.

What is happening?

All of a sudden, the sun disappears behind a black cloud, and a blinding flash of lightning cuts the horizon in two. And then comes an ominous rumble of thunder to shake the unmoving air.

26 The storm strikes the fields

The storm breaks loose over the wheat field. Mercilessly, the wind bends the high stalks; it allows them to straighten up, then crushes them back to the ground.

Sudden lightning, followed by the clap of thunder, illuminates the leaden sky. The fieldmice huddle further into their nest and try to get closer to each other. The lark keeps them company, while the two quails which are hiding nearby cluck anxiously: "You have to be patient and wait until the worst is over."

27 The storm strikes the woods

Because the tall trees are so thick and grow so close together, the woods usually allow only a little sunlight to filter through; and yet the storm manages to penetrate it easily.

A flash of lightning strikes a pine tree and with a dry crack a large branch breaks off, which crashes loudly down onto the soft undergrowth of ferns. The countrymouse, who was sheltering beneath them, only narrowly missed being crushed by it. Luckily, it is very fast and managed to run away, but now it is so terrified that it stands there, petrified, unable to move while everything creaks and groans and moans around it!

Taken by surprise by the storm the little rabbits have not reached the safety of their den, but how can they get to it now? Blinded by the lightning and buffeted by the hailstones, they run wildly, unable to find the way back to their den.

Up in their nest in the pine tree, two little squirrels, even though they are wrapped in their thick tails, find their teeth chattering with the cold. Even the green woodpecker has interrupted his work and waits nervously inside his hole for the storm to vent its fury. What a frightening experience for them all!

28 Thunder in the mountains

The storm is especially fierce high up in the mountains! The rumble of the thunder bounces from rock face to rock face, while the echo is repeated in an endless sequence.

The woodchucks have long ago taken shelter at the bottom of the tunnels in their dens.

Even Snowflake, the young goat, looks for more shelter. The incessant noise of the thunder is terrifying her. So she presses herself as close as possible to her mother. There is no possibility that she will leave her side this time!

29 The multi-colored rainbow

The sky brightens up again. The rumble of the thunder moves off into the distance, growing quieter and quieter until it dies out all together.

A light, steamy mist rises from the fields, and a gentle dripping can be heard all around.

The lark is the first to abandon its hiding place; it shakes the water off its soaking feathers and with its wings spread wide it flies up into the now clear sky. And, while it sings out its joy over the passing of the storm, a rainbow can be seen in an arc of colors and light above the fields.

30 The owl's forecast

On this particular evening, the air is much cooler in the big woods. The deer and his companion, the doe, leap and bound along a rocky gorge carved out of the hillside by the rain water, until they reach the moonlit clearing.

In the middle of the damp grass, rabbits are running around endlessly. With great leaps, the deer chase each other in ever-widening circles. A mouse moves stealthily over a springy bed of moss, soaked in water. After a feast of mushrooms, the squirrels climb up to the top of the fir tree and prepare to go to bed. After the rainfall, large numbers of mushrooms have come out all around the trees and bushes.

And the owl? The wise, old owl who wasn't born yesterday has taken note of the signs and changes which have occurred recently. With its deep, melodious tone, his long, insistent hooting can be heard throughout the forest, and across the countryside. It is a melancholy warning that the summer is soon about to end.

31 The buzzing of the bees

A thick clump of cornflowers has grown by the wall of the orchard: delicate, deep blue flowers, with finely separated petals.

From this clump comes a faint, humming noise: strange, it looks as if there is nothing there! And yet the murmuring continues to spread all around the flowers.

It is the bees! Hundreds of bees, immersed in the blue crowns, busy buzzing and gathering the yellow pollen. And while they are busy with their ceaseless buzzing, they are telling secrets to each other!

1 The queen and her hive

The bees have many secrets, but we can tell you about some of them. First of all, it is easy to find out where they live. Often it is in the trunk of an old chestnut tree, where a hole has been dug out of the bark. They can be seen coming and going endlessly, and it is there that the queen bee has decided to set up the hive, their home. This is a honeycomb of wax cells, all exactly like each other. Yes, the bees do have a queen of their own, and she is the most important member of a swarm of bees.

She is the largest bee in the hive: she commands all the others and is served by them, but the role she plays is very limited. All she has to do is lay eggs, lots of eggs, up to two thousand a day! For this reason, she needs to be very well looked after.

All the other bees are simple "workers", and each group has a precise job to do inside the hive; it is a very hard job which allows them no time for rest all day long.

At the entrance to the hive are the "guards", who prevent enemies and strangers from entering. They do an excellent job as sentries, ready to sting, chase off and even follow intruders, or anything that dares to touch their honey.

2 Twenty thousand busy workers

Let's imagine that you are a bee from the hive, and have free access to move around inside it. The guard bees recognize from your smell that you belong to that hive, since all the bees that belong to it give off the same odor.

Let us enter.

What a busy place it is inside! Thousands and thousands of workers, from twenty to thirty thousand worker bees, incessantly buzzing, are busy doing the work which has been assigned to each group.

We can see bees busy building the hexagonal cones of the hive, with their wax, each one linked to the next; these will later be used both as containers for the honey, and as cribs for the larvae, the newborn bees. Then we find other bees busy cleaning out the cells thoroughly; and still others taking the queen bee her royal jelly, the food that she lives on. Then there are the bees who feed the tiny larvae; and others whose job it is to tidily store the provisions gathered by their companions, the so-called honey bees. And there are also the "ventilator" bees, who beat their wings as fast as they can, in order to keep the beehive cool.

3 Pollen and nectar

From dawn to dusk, a bee flies from flower to flower, choosing the most sweetly scented, breathing in the perfume, which is sometimes subtle and sometimes intense.

Then, very delicately, it gathers the pollen of the flowers, that fine, sweet dust from which bees make honey, and it deposits this in its "baskets" which are positioned at the bottom of each of its legs. The bee also sucks out the nectar from the flowers. This is a very sweet liquid which it gathers in another small container. Back at the hive, it hands over its load, then off it goes again.

4 The honeybee's discovery

That morning the little honeybee was very happy to fly in the clear sunlight, and feel the warm rays caressing its thin, transparent wings. It was so happy that it risked going farther than usual, beyond the big flowering meadow. There, behind a row of hornbeams, it discovered a whole field full of lovely sunflowers.

The bee was amazed. They were so large and majestic, the golden petals of the flowers seemed like living flames licking around a large, velvet heart.

The little honeybee, in a very good mood, immediately went to work. She was so pleased to have come across these exceptionally large flowers that she felt quite giddy from their warm, spicy fragrance.

The bee wanted to tell all her fellow honeybees about her amazing discovery, to let them hear about this precious place as soon as possible, so that they too could come and take their fill of all this pollen and nectar.

So how did she set about telling the other bees about the field of sunflowers? She told them by means of a dance!

5 The dance of the bees

Bees communicate with each other by dancing! As soon as she got back to the hive, the little honeybee placed everything she had gathered into a cell, and then she began a strange dance around the hive, doing full circles, or figure eights, to the right and to the left. She danced and weaved and did pirouettes around and around. The other honeybees watched her and immediately they understood that their companion had found some new, highly perfumed flowers one quarter mile to the north of the hive.

For them that dance was not a mystery, but a very clear message!

6 The uncomfortable stubble

"Oh, that's jagged!" complains the hare, after taking a few leaps into the newly harvested wheat field. Huge machines had cut the wheat and left behind a large yellow carpet of rough and sharp stubble.

"And what's more, I don't feel very safe out here in full sight of everyone. Someone might see me, or they might discover the path I've taken."

"Yes, it's too dangerous," the hare repeats to itself. "What a shame! This wheat field was so safe and secure before it was harvested!"

7 The hare has a different coat

The days are growing shorter. During the night, the air is becoming cooler. A strong wind often moves the pine and larch trees. Giles, the shepherd, has decided it is time to take his flock back down into the valley. The return journey only began yesterday, and it will be made in short stages. No one is in a hurry.

Along the way, the flock can stop and graze in the grassy clearings covered by the last flowers.

Today, after lunch, they have stopped for a rest beside a stream.

Ben, the sheepdog, has allowed the flock to spread out around the sweet-smelling raspberry bushes. Snowflake, the young goat, has set off along a path which leads into the thick of the woods. There she has come face to face with an animal she does not know. It has a round face, with full cheeks and pointed ears. It is a mountain hare.

We know it already. We met it during the spring, when it had a white coat. But during the summer its fur has become brown, so that it will blend better with its surroundings. Nature is very clever to be able to change a hare's coat according to the seasons!

8 The fruit harvest

In Emily's orchard, the harvesting of the fruit has begun. The baskets are all laid out in a line on the grass. The ladder has already been set up against a plum tree, ready for the picking to start.

Usually, Emily does the harvesting by herself, but today she is being helped by Clare, who has come to give her a hand. The work progresses well. Emily deftly picks the fruit off the branches, fills her basket, then passes it down to Clare, who puts the plums into a bigger basket standing on the ground.

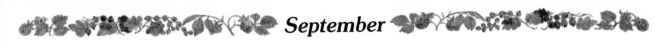

9 Baskets full of ripe plums

After they have finished picking the plums, Clare is going to help Emily in the job of selecting them and preparing them for storage. She is so excited at the thought of helping with this job, that she has come to work in an enormous apron that is too large for her.

"Ah, there you are!" exclaims Emily, as she lets her in. "To start with, you can give the plums a thorough bath in cold water."

"A bath?" asks Clare.

"Yes, a good bath in the sink in lots of clean water."

Clare starts off with enthusiasm. She doesn't mind splashing in the water! The sink is old and made of granite. It is huge, and Clare can only just reach up to the edge. Aunt Emily suggests that she should stand on the small stool which is beside it. When the sink is half full of water, Clare pours in the contents of several baskets and then makes sure the water covers them.

"Rinse the plums one at a time," Emily says. "Those trees were sprayed with insecticide and the fruit must be washed properly."

As she is washing the plums, the water becomes full of dry leaves, blades of grass, flies, and other tiny insects. Clare is amazed. "It didn't look like it, but those plums certainly did need a good bath!" she comments.

Then, following aunt Emily's expert instructions, the little girl begins to take the plums out of the water and put them into a strainer. While carrying them across the floor, she has to be careful not to get it wet, but in the end she does everything successfully!

Afterwards, she lays the fruit out on a large cloth on the table, where the lovely plums are now ready for the next stage in the process.

10 A day for making jam

At last the day has come to make the jam, and Clare is delighted. In a huge copper pot, the plums have already been boiling for hours with just the right amount of sugar added. From time to time, Emily checks how well cooked they all are, basing her judgement on how liquid the mix is as it pours off a wooden spoon. At last, Emily and Clare fill up the glass jars which have been prepared. These are then sealed shut and put into the cupboard from which they will be taken throughout the next year.

11 News about Pudding

Look who is here again! It is Pudding, Clare's sweet, little kitten. Pudding has grown a great deal. During the summer months, with most of its time spent outdoors, it has grown strong and its lovely fur now shines like silk. As far as its character is concerned, it is still the same Pudding as before: amusing, extremely playful, and mischievous.

Its favorite pastime is still chasing butterflies, and the ever-active kitten leaps about tirelessly all over the place. Clare thinks Pudding is the best kitten in the world!

12 Coralbeak flies away

Coralbeak and his mate, the two exotic birds, spend their summer in a large bird cage set up beside the glass doors which lead out into the garden of the house.

The window, which is almost always open, lets in a lot of air and light, along with the delicate perfume of the flowers and the songs of the birds which live in the trees and bushes of the garden.

The two, exotic, little birds seem to be very happy in their lovely cage. They cheerfully twitter from morning till night, and hungrily peck at their food, and make short rapid flights from one perch to another. Coralbeak is very restless and very lively, while his companion, on the other hand, is very calm.

Aunt Sophia takes very good care of the cage and not a day goes by without her cleaning it out thoroughly. She puts new sand on the bottom, she changes the water in the little bowls and fills the food dish with fresh food. The two little birds are used to her calm movements, to her soft, gentle voice, and so they keep calm during her visits. Always that is, except for this particular morning, when Coralbeak could contain his curiosity no longer, and flew out of the cage, taking advantage of a moment when Sophia opened the door to put in a piece of biscuit. Attracted by the loud chirping from the woods, Coralbeak, flaps his wings and dashes out into the large, sunlit garden.

Out there, everything seems huge! And the little bird has to beat its wings extra hard to cross the open space and find somewhere to land.

All alone in the cage, Coralbeak's mate cried in a sad but melodious song. She cannot accept that she has been left all alone.

Will Coralbeak return?

13 Coralbeak in the garden

The exotic little bird's adventure outside the cage soon becomes an endless series of mishaps.

To begin with, Coralbeak is dazzled by the sunlight which seems so bright to him. Then he is bewildered by the deafening noises of all the other birds. And these birds seem very large and unfriendly to him!

As soon as he lands on the grass, a blackbird appears before him, with a large yellow beak which looks menacing. Coralbeak scuttles for shelter into a large cluster of daisies.

14 The dark, frightening night

Coralbeak ends up spending the first part of the night between two large dahlias. Because he is so used to the warmth of the house and to having his companion beside him, the little bird feels cold, and afraid, and he is also hungry; so hungry because out here he doesn't have the dish, filled with fresh food, that he is used to, and in this unknown garden he certainly isn't capable of finding food by himself.

After midnight, he wakens, stiff and drowsy, drinks a few drops of dew and tries pecking at some blades of grass. But he gives that up immediately, because the grass is too bitter!

The dark is not at all pleasant for poor Coralbeak. He has never been outside at night before and the strange noises of the creatures moving frighten him. He hops nervously from one perch to another, feeling ill at ease on all of them.

In the end, more by luck than by judgement, the little bird manages to reach the window ledge of his house, and there he settles down, afraid to even move any more. In fact, he is very lucky indeed because, during the night, a big, grey cat comes very close to making a tasty titbit out of him!

15 All's well that ends well

During Coralbeak's absence, his companion back in the cage has not stopped uttering loud, sharp calls. Dawn is just breaking, when Coralbeak at last hears these calls, and, guided by them, he finds his way to the window of the room.

The next morning, aunt Sophia finds the fugitive, shocked but safe and sound, outside the glass doors. She immediately picks him up and puts him back in the cage. Coralbeak has never been so pleased to be inside his cage. All's well that ends well!

16 Catching flies for a frog

How is the green frog doing, the one that Jane gave to Andrew as a present last April? Has it grown used to its new life? Is it now used to living in a glass bowl?

It seems to be quite happy. It continually climbs up and down the miniature ladder which the children put inside the transparent bowl. For no reason at all, it will jump up in the air, as if it was on a spring. It is always alert and ready to hop.

Andrew, on the other hand, has lost a little of his first enthusiasm. He still likes the frog, but, to be honest, he is tired of looking after it. This is partly due to the fact that the frog eats nothing but flies, and, what's more, live ones! Andrew is kept very busy trying to catch them.

Of course, if the frog was free to catch the food for itself, it would have no trouble hunting the flies, and it could even vary its diet, adding mosquitoes, water fleas and other insects which live in hordes around the edges of the pond. But, there, in that strange glass house, the frog has to make do with flies.

So, as soon as Andrew hears the slight buzzing of a fly, he waits until he spots his prey, then he tries to catch it in flight, or set a trap, such as catching it in the curtains or confusing it on the window pane. As soon as he catches it, he holds onto it in the hollow of his hands, and then Andrew hurries over to place it in the glass bowl.

The frog immediately leaps forwards on its long legs and grabs the buzzing insect out of the air. But then it seems to say: "Is that all?" So Andrew can do nothing but go and look for another fly, and then another one. And the same goes on all day long, seven days a week. Finally, Andrew decides to put the frog back in the pond where it first came from.

17 A frog goes home

Andrew goes back to the banks of the pond, among the reeds, with his sister Jane. He puts the glass bowl down on the grass and, very slowly, he takes off the gauze he had put across the top to close it.

The frog doesn't wait to be asked. It immediately jumps out onto the grass. From there, one leap at a time, it makes its way into the water, creating a series of concentric circles on its smooth surface which slowly spread out across the pond. Andrew and Jane look at each other: "It's gone!" They agree: "It will be a lot happier now!"

18 The signs of summer's end

The first meadow saffrons are coming out. They are a pale violet color, and they dot the fields. By this time, they are practically the only flowers, and they are also the last ones of the season. Everyone feels a little sad when they begin to appear, because their arrival announces that the summer is about to end.

But there is also another reason why the meadow saffrons are not a very well-loved flower. They are poisonous and it is not very wise to pick them. So it is not only because it is a messenger of autumn that this flower causes us to sigh.

19 The swallows get ready to leave

"There seem to be hundreds of them!" shouts Clare, looking at the long row of swallows daintily perched on the electricity wires.

"No, there aren't more than a hundred!" her brother Mark corrects her. "Well then, a hundred" accepts Clare sulkily. "But that's still a lot. I wonder what they are doing up on the electricity wire."

Over the last few days, the familiar swallows have been coming together in larger numbers on the high voltage wires. And there they all engage in a constant twittering, spending hours and hours conferring with each other, nodding their heads and waving their forked tails.

"I know what they are saying to each other," Mark says, not wanting his sister to remain puzzled. "The swallows are making plans for their journey."

"What journey?" asks Clare.

"Their return trip," answers Mark. "As soon as they feel the first cold spells, the swallows will head south to spend the winter in warm countries. Right now, they are all discussing the date of departure, the route they will follow, what stops they should make, and into how many flocks they should split up. In fact, I am sure that they are preparing for their long flight of migration in great detail."

20 The autumn equinox

After the spring equinox, the night of March 20th-21st, when the day and the night are of the same length, there comes the autumn equinox. The combined forces of attraction of the sun and the moon cause the highest tides of the season. Like a huge broom, the sea sweeps up on all the beaches. Down come the last sand-castles, a reminder of the summer, while the waves break upon piers, rocks and breakwaters, and cause the equinox storms.

All the seabirds shout together: "Goodbye, summer, goodbye!"

During the summer the fruits ripen in the woods: the fresh redcurrants, the sweet raspberries, the succulent strawberries. To go out and pick them is a real delight! They are delicious to eat, and it is a lot of fun making them into jam to be eaten in the winter.

Redcurrants

Raspberries

Strawberries

What would you choose from such a tempting basket? A velvety peach, a ripe apricot, a sweet plum, or that raspberry all on its own?

Summer at the seaside is always full of discoveries; lots of crabs and little fish, lots of seaweed and seashells!

The sea gulls fish on the surface of the water. They make wide circles as they come down to land on the beach, and they fill the sky with their shrill cries.

Sea gull

Crab

In the summer, there is an explosion of warm, bright colors. The
butterfly flutters around happily, completely carefree; the lizard
warms itself in the sun, but is always ready to flee at the first sign
of danger.

Lizard

In the summer on the high mountain meadows, the little woodchucks search for the sweetest and most juicy flowers, but they are very careful that the eagle doesn't get too close!

Eagle

Woodchuck

During the summer, the chamois graze freely along the steep, grassy slopes, climbing nimbly up and down sheer rock faces.

Chamois

In summer, vases are filled bursting with flowers! There is such a variety to choose from; roses, asters, carnations, zinnias, dahlias, marigolds, hollyhocks, and who knows how many other flowers!

A summer wild flower collection

Mallow

Buttercup

Bellflower

Cornflower

Contents

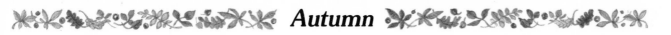

The mice and the missing ring

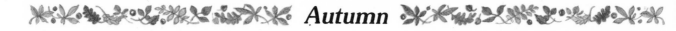

Nicola has gone for a few days to visit her grandparents in their house in the country, a lovely, old home, the front of which is all covered by vines, that turn a lovely, bright, red color this time of year.

She is going to stay with her grandparents for a few days, until school starts again. As soon as she arrives, she runs straight to her bedroom, the one set aside for guests, the brightest room in a rather grim and austere house. The walls are covered in bright wallpaper, and there is a happy, flowery pattern on the bed-spread and curtains. On the bedside table, there is a lovely vase of flowers to welcome her: grandmother always puts these out when Nicola comes to stay.

Her grandparents are very kind to her and Nicola enjoys coming to stay in their big, old house. Best of all, she likes her grandmother, Alice, who tells her about all the amazing things that have happened during her lifetime. This evening, for example, she tells her a really fascinating story. Granny had been reminded of it by grandpa, who was complaining about all the mice that roam the house in the fall.

It was an incident which happened to granny many years ago, one of the first times she ever came to that house, even before she got married to Nicola's grandpa, Tony.

"I liked this house at once," granny Alice says, abandoning herself to her memories. "The big window let in a lot of light, along with bird songs and fragrances from the garden. The house was a bit grim, that's true, with its heavy, dark furniture, but it was brightened up by nice cotton curtains with pretty patterns, and, most of all, by flowers, in vases all over the place."

"I was to stay in the guest room on the first floor. Frances, my future sister-in-law, had prepared it especially for me. She had chosen the nicest flowers and put them in a porcelain vase. On the bedside table there was a jug of water with a glass beside it; she had even remembered to put some bags of fragrant lavender in the closet; and, on the desk, there was a basket full of fruits of the season."

"I was very pleased with the warm welcome I was given," continued granny Alice, "and before I went to bed I had another look at the lovely engagement ring I had just been given by Anthony; then I took it off and put it on the bedside table."

"As soon as I woke up the next morning I reached out my hand to pick up the ring. I could not find it immediately, so I got out of bed to take

a better look. There was no sign of the ring. I rubbed my eyes, but the ring was definitely not there. It had disappeared."

"I thought that it might have fallen on the floor: but no, it wasn't there either. I began to get more and more frantic in my search: I looked under the bed, in the closet, under the rugs, but all to no avail. I became desperate! I couldn't believe it. "It isn't possible," I said to myself. "A ring cannot just disappear!"

"I hurriedly got dressed and rushed off to look for Anthony. I told him what had happened and how surprised and unhappy I was about this mysterious

disappearance."

"In no time at all, the whole family was gathered in my room, searching for the ring. We all searched high and low, but still we couldn't find it."

"My future mother-in-law tried to reassure me: "My dear Alice, I can assure you there are no ghosts in this house!"

"At that point, I had an idea," continued granny Alice. "I thought that perhaps a mouse might have taken the ring."

"Yes, at this time of year the mice go on raids all over the house," admitted my future father-in-law. "But I don't think it's possible that the mice

could have taken a ring."

"The whole family had the same opinion," said granny Alice. "But in the end, just to make me happy, they all admitted that it just might be possible. I thought, in fact, that a mouse might have taken my ring while it was out gathering supplies for the winter. Mice do pick up odds and ends, like buttons and pieces of paper, along with edible items. Perhaps an enterprising mouse had come into my room during the night, and been attracted by my splendid new ring, and taken it off my bedside table."

"And so we all began to take a closer look at every possible hole in the wall. And, there, behind the chest of drawers, we found one. Anthony's father gave us permission to remove some of the plaster, and, to everyone's amazement, we discovered a long tunnel, at the end of which was the nest of the mice. And there, in the middle of lots of different bits and pieces, my shining ring stood out!"

This story absolutely enchanted Nicola. And tonight, under her lovely warm quilt, the little girl will surely dream about granny's romantic story: her arrival in the old country house, all those flowers, all those smiles... but also all those little mice around her engagement ring!

21 A sign of autumn

Elizabeth suddenly realizes she is very late for school. If she wants to get there in time she is going to have to take a short cut through the park.

On her way, something hard lands suddenly on her head with a thud, and then rolls off in front of her.

Rubbing her head, Elizabeth bends over to pick up the chestnut which has dropped from the horse-chestnut tree.

"Autumn really is here now," she thinks. "I'll show this chestnut to the teacher!" And she places the little chestnut in her school bag.

22 A bag full of chestnuts

"Hello, mom," says Matthew brightly, on his return from school.

"Hello, dear," answers his mother, without raising her head from her knitting. But then she asks: "How was your day at school? Did you have a test? How did your homework go? If you want something to eat, there is fruit in the kitchen."

When, at last, his mother raises her eyes from her knitting, she exclaims in surprise: "What a full bag you have! How did you manage to carry such a heavy weight? When you left this morning, I didn't notice that it was so full!" Matthew's bag is filled to bursting point. Its sides are stretched and bulging out, and the straps seem to be ready to give way. But from the shape of the bulges, it is obvious that it is not full of books!

Matthew pretends at first that there is nothing unusual about his bag, but then he admits that he has brought home a bag full of newly-fallen chestnuts, some dark, shiny brown, others still inside their green, spiky cases. He has gathered them on his way home from beneath the big horse-chestnut tree.

23 A carpet of golden leaves

The wind has stopped. The heavy rainstorm which had come after it has moved on, leaving behind a lovely, clear sky.

The sides of the road are now covered in big leaves. They are the large leaves of the horse-chestnut, made up of seven, individual leaves, each of which spreads out from a single point.

As the autumn days go by, the green color of the leaves slowly gives way to a golden yellow. More and more leaves fall, until the grey surface of the road has been transformed into a vast golden carpet.

24 Different types of chestnuts

Matthew's mother has made a very special dessert for dinner this evening. It is sweet and creamy, with a deliciously different flavor.

"What is this called?" asks Matthew.

"It is a marron glace. It is made from chestnuts and sugar. This is also called candied chestnuts," replies his mom.

"Do you mean that this is made out of all those chestnuts I collected?" asks Matthew in great excitement.

"No! I'm afraid not," his mother calms him down. "The chestnuts you collected come from the horse-chestnut tree, and they are not good to eat. They are very bitter. The chestnuts in a marron glace, and the chestnuts that we gather for roasting come from the common chestnut tree. Common chestnut trees have huge branches and grow up above 600 feet in altitude, in the mountains."

"With their delicious chestnuts, we make marron glace, which is often given as a gift in many countries at Christmas time. Common chestnuts are wonderful and they taste just great after being roasted over a charcoal grill on the street corner, or in the oven at home."

25 A house of fallen leaves

A strong wind had been blowing in heavy gusts all night. The next morning the garden is covered in leaves. They are all over the place; along the paths, on the lawn and in the shrubs. Clare and Mark's mother don't like to see a mess like that.

"Children, please go out and pick up all those leaves."

Mark and Clare were playing and they don't really feel like working, but they do as their mother tells them. They get the rakes out of the garden shed and they begin piling the leaves up into small piles. Then, bit by bit, Mark drags them all together into one big heap underneath the tree.

"What shall we do with them now?" Clare asks.

"I've got an idea," says Mark. "Let's make a leaf house out of them."

"A house?" asks Clare in surprise. "And what shall we do with it?"

"Give me a hand and you'll see," Mark says. "Gather them up and press them down hard to make the house walls. Good, now we can go inside without knocking the whole thing over."

"We can use it for the next treasure hunt," Clare suggests eagerly.

"What a good idea!" exclaims Mark, putting the final touches to the leaf house.

26 Ducks in trouble

Every day the sun is rising a little later, and its rays are growing weaker and weaker. A cool breeze blows through the reeds, disturbing the surface of the water in the pond.

Bit by bit, the lilies are losing their color, and all around in the woods the leaves on the trees are turning yellow.

For a few days now, the seven little, wild ducks in the pond have been behaving strangely. They are restless and depressed; not as lively as they usually are.

A graceful dragonfly is flying about nearby, but they no longer stick out their beaks and try to pluck it out of the air the way they used to. Even when a frog hops past them, they do not attempt to chase after it.

During the afternoon trip, the liveliest of the ducklings decides to go further than usual, as far as the mill. But then he finds that no matter how hard he beats his wings, he is unable to take off and fly! He doesn't even have the strength to lift off from the ground! To make things worse he finds that all the flapping is causing large clumps of his feathers to fall out!

A truly pitiful situation! All the other wild ducks, his brothers and sisters, find themselves with the same problems.

So, depressed and filled with shame, the ducks slink off and hide behind the reeds, in among the swamp grasses. And that is where the mother duck finds them. She immediately begins to try and cheer them up.

She explains gently the reasons they are having these problems. She tells them: "Every year wild ducks lose their feathers when the autumn comes, just as I do. But don't worry, they will soon grow back more shiny and healthy than ever. Then, you will be able to take off in flight again and begin your journey towards warmer countries, where we will spend the winter."

27 Strange noises in the forest

The little hare born during the summer among the honeysuckle bushes has turned into a fine adult: long legs, big ears and a thick brown coat which allows it to blend in with its surroundings. It has its den under a pine tree in the woods, but it often comes out to wander around in the surrounding fields.

The hare knows its territory very well, all the sounds and smells. But just now it is a little worried. During the past week, it has been hearing strange, alarming noises in the forest: scratching, scraping and thuds!

28 The harlequin hedgehog

"What is this strange, little animal, about the size of an apple?" Mark wonders as he sees it approaching alongside the garden wall.

It turns out to be the hedgehog, the one that used to come in the spring and drink the milk that Mark and Clare kept outside the kitchen door. It is coming back from its nocturnal visit to the orchard. The falling leaves from the pear and plum trees have become stuck onto the prickles of its back, making it look as if it's wearing a harlequin's cloak.

29 An explanation for the noises

The endless noises from the forest continue to alarm the young hare, which is now ready to jump out of his skin at the first sound.

What is that rustling noise that he can hear coming from behind him?

Perhaps it is a dead leaf which has fallen onto other dead leaves?

And what is that unusual, thudding sound?

Perhaps it is a pine cone rolling down the hill?

And what is that continuous scratching noise?

Could it be a branch moving in the strong, autumn wind?

What about that scraping sound?

Perhaps it is the sound of acorns falling to the ground?

There must be a simple explanation for all these strange sounds. The hare is still very apprehensive, nevertheless. But he takes comfort from the fact that one thing is happening which is to his advantage: a thick mist is forming!

He is so grateful for these thin, white tendrils which cover the countryside. Now the hare can run across the fields and meadows with no fear of being seen! And he can find his way easily by sniffing his old trails. Thanks to this mist, friend and accomplice, he can even get into the village orchard during the daytime!

30 A well-dressed gathering

A long leafy branch on the chestnut tree has been chosen as a meeting place by the hoopoes from the woods.

It is certainly a very well-dressed meeting! Hoopoes have pink-brown plumage, boldly striped black and white wings and crests on their heads which would do credit to a Red Indian, with black tips to the feathers.

But what a noisy assembly! All the birds twitter at the same time. It is, of course, a very important meeting. The hoopoes are discussing the date of their departure for Africa.

1 Food for the squirrels

There is a nice surprise for everyone today. On the big nut trees at the edge of the woods, amid the round, jagged-edged leaves, pairs of soft green pods containing large nuts have appeared.

As soon as the mother squirrel sees them, she calls her young out to harvest them immediately. This is a source of rich food that the squirrels must quickly take advantage of.

Crack, crack, crack! One after another, the empty shells fall to the ground. "What a feast," the little squirrels say to each other.

2 Bunches of juicy grapes

The children have come to the country to visit their aunt. They are always happy to go and see her as she always welcomes them with a lovely smile in her bright, blue eyes, and instantly makes them feel at home.

The two children are able to go out in the open air whenever they choose. And the day they arrive, after their afternoon snack, the children wander out into the garden.

As usual, when they are outside, they all want to do different things at the same time. They pause for a moment to take a closer look at a row of little fat plants surrounding a big cactus in a corner of the garden. Then they are off towards the olives growing on the sloping land further down. Then they stick their hands and arms into the big stone water tub. And finally they race off towards the neat rows of vines.

At this time of year, the grapes are almost ripe, and the big, juicy bunches look very tempting. The children would like to break some off, but they don't dare. However, when it is time for them to leave, their aunt gives them a basket filled with black and green grapes that she has picked just for them.

3 The badger loves grapes

The badger also loves grapes! At night, it often leaves its den in the woods to go and look for a row of vines, loaded with juicy bunches of grapes. It will waddle along until it finds a vine of lovely black grapes hanging down low. Then, bunch by bunch, it harvests a lot! The badger is very greedy; almost as if it has decided to go on a diet of grapes alone!

When it is satisfied, this fine-looking mammal, with its distinctive black and white head, ambles back to its den, where it will go to sleep and dream of further visits to the vineyard!

4 The hedgehogs' moonlight feast

A chilly autumn wind has been blowing all day, only easing off as evening falls, and the moon begins to rise in the sky.

The pears in the orchard, which are nearly ripe, have been blown by the wind, and a large number of them have fallen off and landed on the grass below.

This is a very happy time for all the hedgehogs in the neighborhood! They all make their way slowly into the orchard, where, with pears for everyone, they have a happy feast in the moonlight.

5 Everyone's favorite fruit, the apple

The apple is one of the most loved fruit trees, and it has a lot of friends. During the spring, the apple tree becomes covered in delicate, pink colored flowers which are a joy to behold. They lighten everyone's heart with their promise that every flower will become a fruit. And in the autumn, the branches of the tree will be filled with lots of red, yellow or green apples.

During this season, the birds which regularly visit it find shiny, colored apples and, after a whole lot of chirping and twittering, whole flocks of them gorge themselves on this delicious fruit. Their tiny beaks go to work like a lot of little scalpels, cutting into the sweet, juicy pulp.

During the night, other visitors wander around on the leaf-covered grass beneath the trees. There are country mice, hedgehogs and fieldmice. They spend hours and hours slowly moving around the trunk in search of something to eat. They are looking for apples which have fallen off the tree. And as soon as their sharp eyes spot one half buried in the grass, they begin immediately with gusto: crunch, crunch, crunch! Their razor sharp teeth cut, chew and chomp. In no time at all, only the core of the apple is left.

What about children? They love apples as much as anyone and they come looking for them at all hours of the day. The bigger ones often climb up into the tree and pick the nicest apples they can find. But before they bite into them, they know that they must first wash them. It is not good enough just to wipe them.

All shiny and bright after they have been cleaned, apples look really delicious. They can be eaten bite by bite, or they can be cut into halves or into slices. Whatever way you eat it, an apple is always good for you.

6 "Goodbye, dear swallows..."

"It is sad to see the nest completely empty," sighs Clare, as she closes the door to the shed behind her.

"And to think that they had repaired it completely and even enlarged it," comments Mark, who always looks on the practical side of things.

"I wonder," continues Clare, "why they left; and where they've gone."

"I know that every year they leave and the following year they return; but I don't know how it is that they find their way back," says Mark, puzzled.

"It will be nice if they come back," sighs Clare. "It will be especially nice if the same birds come back!"

"Let's go out and look for James," suggests Mark: "He knows all about flowers, and he also knows a lot of things about animals. He'll know about the swallows' comings and goings!"

Mark and Clare find the gardener in the greenhouse, busy with his pots and his plants. He is a rather cranky character, but he always answers the children's questions. He listens carefully to what they have to say, as usual, and then explains: "The swallows leave in the autumn because, with the approach of winter, those insects that they live on disappear. They don't want to die of hunger, so they have to migrate to warmer countries, where the insects are always abundant."

"We saw them a few days ago perched on the electricity wires and they all looked as if they were getting ready to leave," declares Clare. "I wonder if they are still on those wires?"

"No, they haven't been there for a few days now," says Mark.

The children become thoughtful, while James gets on with his work, without paying any more attention to them. All of a sudden, Clare shouts: "Look, up there! There's a whole flock of swallows flying over us now! They really are leaving. Goodbye, dear swallows. See you next year! Goodbye for now!"

7 The swallows' long journey

Clare is still curious about certain things concerning the swallows, but this time she decides to go and ask her aunt for the answers.

"In the autumn, the swallows undertake an amazing journey to get to the warm countries where they spend the winter," explains her aunt, opening the atlas. "Look, the swallows cross the Mediterranean, they pass over the Sahara desert and fly on down into the center of Africa."

"But will they come back in the spring?" Clare wants to know.

"Yes, without fail, the swallows will return to the same place again every spring!"

8 The ducks' new outfits

There is wonder and joy at the pond. The young ducks have become completely covered in new feathers!

All their unhappiness is forgotten! All their tiredness has vanished!

Just look at them now, happily preening their new feathers, and admiring their new outfits, and their bright shiny reflections in the water.

The four young ducks now have feathers of a delicate pastel brown color, just like those of their mother. The three young drakes each have a fine collar of emerald-green feathers, just like their father.

9 Birds on the beach

The lively shouts of children and their noisy games have disappeared from the beach. Like a whole flock of birds taking flight, they had to accept finally, with heavy hearts, that it was time to leave the seaside and go back to school.

The young shrimp-fishers, the shell collectors, the crab and mussel hunters, the ones who loved diving from the rocks, they have all disappeared, as if by magic.

But this doesn't mean that the long stretches of sand have been left silent and empty. In place of the children, there has now arrived a whole host of migrating birds from the Scandinavian countries, which will spend the long winter months in this milder climate.

There are plovers with their golden-yellow plumage and their flute-like calls; the turnstones, with their bright orange legs, constantly turning over pebbles and gravel in search of worms and shellfish; and then there are the oyster-catchers, who are always looking for oysters; and the curlews, with their long curved beaks and sweet song.

Together, all these birds liven up the beaches, just as much, or even more, than all those noisy, carefree playing children.

10 How swallows sleep at sea

The swallows have been flying now for several days over a countryside already weathered in dull, autumn colors. Exhausted, they stop to rest at night. At dawn, they begin again and fly higher and higher, their wings flapping strongly. The land of the sun is still a long way away!

Today, they have been flying constantly over a sea that is alight with blue, green, and violet reflections.

But where will they stop to sleep at night? They will fly down and settle on the bridge of some ship.

11 Formation flying

If you should happen to be beside the large pond in the rosy light of dawn, you might see a flock of birds approaching, flying in an arrowhead formation.

It is a flock of wild ducks on their journey towards warmer countries. For several days now, dozens of ducks have been landing on the calm sheet of water which extends from the reed-covered edges of the pond. They land there to rest; and for a short time the air is raucous with the sounds of their quacking.

The seven young ducks who have always lived on the pond are attracted to all this excitement. Without a second thought, they go and join the new arrivals. They swim alongside them, and they also follow them in flight above the reeds, and share with them the last snails and the tufts of tasty watercress.

But in the end, at dawn one morning, the travelers take off for the last time and head away into the distance, with the best flier leading them. Three of the young wild ducks take off after them, leaving behind the pond where they were born. They join the arrowhead formation for an exciting journey into the unknown.

12 Beaver is my name!

I wear a fur coat of the very best quality, very, very soft, with silvery reflections. It is warm and waterproof.

I am fairly large and I weigh quite a lot. My eyes are small, but to make up for that, my ears and my nose are very keen. When I dive into the water, they close automatically.

I love swimming, and so I spend most of my time in the water. To help me swim better, I have an excellent pair of flippers, which are really my back legs. My strong, flat tail acts as my rudder.

As you can see, I am perfectly equipped for swimming underwater, and for traveling along different types of waterways.

But I still haven't mentioned my front legs, which are almost like two real hands. They allow me to hold very small objects.

And I must not forget my teeth, my most important tools. They are so strong and sharp, that I can even cut through tree trunks with them, just like a real woodcutter.

I hope that you have some understanding now of what it means to be a beaver!

13 The beaver's lodge

It would be very difficult for any one of us to pay a visit to a beaver at his home, which is called a lodge. For a start, it is hidden under the surface of the water.

To get into his lodge, the beaver first has to swim down to the bottom of the river or the lake. There he enters into a long corridor, which ends inside his lodge. When he arrives there, the beaver stops for a minute in the hall, to shake the water off; then he enters into the large, comfortable main room of his house.

14 The beaver's dam

The chamber of the beaver's lodge, the largest room in its house, is very comfortable. It has a nice, dry floor, covered by a bed of wooden twigs and pieces of bark, and a tall ventilation shaft, so it is well aired.

The whole beaver family lives safely in this house. The beaver built it all himself, and he also built the big dam which crosses the river from one side to the other.

Made of finely woven branches and of dried mud, the purpose of this barrier is to protect the beaver's house, and keep the entrance always hidden under water, even during periods of drought.

To build their dams, beavers chop down poplars and birch trees, cutting branches and stumps. Of course, all this wood is too heavy to carry. So how does the beaver solve this problem? It digs a whole series of channels through which it floats the wood, and, without too much effort, the beaver brings the wood back to the site of the dam. The beaver is one of nature's most tireless and ingenious builders.

15 The beaver's dinner menu

The beaver has a healthy appetite. It is as tireless and expert in the art of obtaining food for itself and its family, as it is in the art of building.

This extraordinary animal knows how to use its strong teeth to break up and shape the bark of the willow, poplar and birch trees. To this, the main dish, it then adds tender vegetables, aquatic plants, soft water-lily roots, willow leaves and flowers. And then, for dessert, the beaver is very good at finding apples, pears or other seasonal fruits.

16 The woodchucks make hay

I am sure that it will not surprise you very much to learn that woodchucks make their beds out of hay. Lots of animals use hay for their beds. However, it might surprise you if I tell you that woodchucks make their own hay!

Towards the end of the summer, these stout, burrowing animals gather lots of blades of grass, which are then chewed a little. All these blades of grass are laid out in the sun on the tops of large rocks, and, when they are dry, the woodchucks carry the hay down into their dens to make soft, fragrant beds.

17 A change in the scenery

There is a chill in the air now, but the climb warms them. Anna and her cousin Mary have decided to climb up to the high mountain meadows once more, the kingdom of the woodchucks, before the end of the season.

When they reach the top of the slope, they stop to catch their breath beside a large rock which hides them from sight. From there they take in the views of the surrounding countryside.

"I really don't recognize anything anymore!" says Anna in disappointment. "The landscape is completely different. There are no more flowers, the sky is grey and sad, and the mountains are overcast by those low clouds which cover their summits!"

"That's because it is autumn now," her cousin Mary points out.

"But where have the woodchucks gone?" asks Anna, even more disappointed.

"They must already be in their dens, where they are getting their beds ready for their long winter sleep," says her cousin.

"What do you mean?" asks Anna.

"Those thick bundles of hay, that they dragged down their tunnels, and laid out in piles, will be getting pressed down properly now. The woodchucks really need to make sure it is comfortable since it will be their bedroom for the whole winter."

18 Everyone inside, we're closing up!

The decision has been made! It is time to close the door to the den. It is time to go into hibernation.

Friends and families all get together to say goodbye, looking forward to seeing each other next spring. And then they each go to their own homes.

Now the clever woodchucks have to seal the entrance to their den thoroughly. To do this, they put stones, earth, and pebbles against it, all obtained from a little "mine" they had previously dug out. When the last stone is in place, they really are cut off from the world.

19 Good night and sweet dreams!

Now that the work has been finished, the woodchucks finally get ready to go to sleep; and to do this they cuddle next to each other, buried up to their necks in the warm and sweet-smelling hay.

Tubby and round as they are, the woodchucks don't have much room in the den. But that's all for the best; the reserve of fat they have built up during the summer will give them the strength to live through their winter hibernation. In the spring, however, they will be a lot thinner, and then there will be too much room in the den!

20 The squirrels fill up their cabinets

The sudden rainstorms, the more frequent shroud of fog, the chilly wind, and the cold nights do not stop the squirrels, who are still at the height of their activity, from rummaging through even the most hidden corners of the woods.

For days and days now, they have been busy gathering provisions for the winter months. Even the youngsters have to help: for them it is just a new game to add to all the others.

Of course, for the young ones who were born last spring, this type of work is totally new. However, by closely watching their parents, their brothers and sisters, and all the other adults in the group, they soon learn how to imitate them naturally. You should see how eagerly and how well they take part in this collective task.

Their favorite game has become digging up all types of seeds! They continually challenge each other to find the biggest nuts, the freshest pine cones, the hardest beans, and the crunchiest acorns.

Having built up an abundant supply of food, the squirrels now have the problem of where to put it, how to find a suitable storage space. But the squirrels do not give up easily and they soon find many places for food cabinets, perfect for this purpose. They can make use of a hole in the trunk of a pine tree, or a hollow in the roots of a beech tree, or even an old, abandoned nest.

Now everything is ready; let the winter come! But the squirrels do have one worry: will they be able to remember all the hiding places where they have hoarded their supplies?

Of course they'll remember! When the biting cold has paralyzed the whole forest, when the squirrels are driven by a gnawing hunger, the clever adult ones will soon be able to find these precious supplies.

21 The golden forest

"What a lovely day!" says Clare's mother, entranced by the sight of her garden bathed in a golden light that softens the outlines of everything in it. "I love the autumn. Today the weather is perfect for a walk in the woods."

And so, in the early hours of the afternoon, Clare and her mother walk along the path which leads into the forest. At first, the path winds through some fields and as they pass, large quails, fearing themselves threatened, fly out of their way, while the skylarks take off in steep, rapid flights and sing their afternoon songs.

As soon as they enter into the woods, Clare and her mother find themselves in the midst of a deep silence, only occasionally broken by the rustling of the leaves breaking off from the trees and gently falling to the ground. All around them, it is as if a golden rain has covered everything: trees, branches, leaves, ferns, and mosses. And it even seems that as they fall, the leaves take on golden reflections before they reach the ground. Enchanted by this magical atmosphere, Clare and her mother keep absolutely silent so they don't break the spell.

22 Hide and seek in the ferns

In the woods, the leaves of many trees and bushes have turned red.

The ferns, fretted like precious lace work, have become a warm, gold color and they rustle like delicately waving fans when the light breeze catches them. The singular sound momentarily surprises two little rabbits who are passing through the tall, fern plants.

One of the rabbits leaps to one side and hides behind a curtain of ferns. But the other one spots the white tail of his friend and leaps after him into the lacy, golden-yellow ferns. Got you!

And now it is his turn to hide.

Quickly he ducks under a clump of small bushes, where he huddles down under a leafy branch and keeps absolutely still...

All of a sudden, he hears something else moving about on this carpet of leaves, and a moment later a beast with a pointed muzzle is leaping towards him! It's a weasel! It had been so well camouflaged among the leaves that the little rabbit did not spot it until almost too late. And he only just manages to make his escape in time.

His other little rabbit friend also gets out of there as fast as he can!

23 An autumn collage

"I want to make my room look prettier," announces Clare enthusiastically. She decides to make an ornamental collage out of the collection of leaves she has gathered over the last few days.

Having laid them out artistically, Clare glues all the leaves, from different trees, varied in shape and size, onto a large sheet of paper. The finished collage has large palm-shaped leaves from the horse-chestnut, and elongated, thin ones from the willow; then oak leaves, poplar and maple leaves, each with its own special autumnal beauty.

24 The nutshell fleet

A raging storm and strong winds stop Mark and Clare from going out. The children grow bored in silence. They had planned to go for a ride on their bicycles, perhaps their last chance this year, or else go for a game of tag with their friends, and maybe even play some other games with them. But all their plans have to be changed. What can they do?

"Why don't you build yourselves some little ships?" suggests their mother.

"Ships?" Mark and Clare look at her blankly.

"Is it all this water falling out of the sky," Mark says jokingly, "is that what is making you think about ships?"

"No, I got the idea from looking at that basket of nuts on the table," says their mother.

Mark and Clare look at each other perplexed, but their mother has already gone to work. She breaks some nuts exactly in half, then she takes the shells, sticks a match into the center of each one, gluing it with a drop of wax. The match is to be the ship's mast! To it she sticks a piece of colored paper: that is the sail.

Now they all get busy breaking open nuts. After a while, they have a large fleet, which for a while uses the bookshelves as its harbor.

25 Matthew flies his kite

A heavy, gusty wind makes Matthew want to fly his kite outside. "Well done, wind! Blow as hard as you can; take my kite high up into the sky," Matthew says to himself, enthusiastically, as he starts running across the fields, slowly letting out the cord like a real expert.

But, after several upward swoops and downward nose dives, the kite is having trouble gaining height. Finally, though, it flies way up into the sky. Matthew shouts at it: "Higher, higher!" and he races breathlessly along behind his kite, which is soaring up above him.

26 The majestic, white swan

White and proud, the splendid, young swan glides slowly over the calm waters of the lake. What a difference from last spring!

Then it was a clumsy, grey, little cygnet, with large, protruding eyes and uncoordinated movements, and now it has changed into a magnificent swan with pure white feathers and a regal way of moving. All the ducks maintain a proper distance, out of admiration. They look at it with respect and they seem to grow smaller and smaller in the presence of such majesty, hiding themselves behind the reeds.

27 The moorhen and the frogs

Hop, hop, hop! The moorhen skims over the surface of the water in the pond, swiftly pattering from one water-lily to the next.

It is going down to where the fresh water flows and the watercress is abundant. There it will meet the frogs and tell them all the latest news from the pond.

As she approaches, the moorhen cannot see the frogs. They are probably dozing on the bottom of the pond. But when the moorhen arrives, the frogs become alert, and all croak together impatiently: "Tell us the news!"

"Well, we received a visit from a squirrel!" the moorhen informs her audience. "It wanted to reach the nut trees on the other side and decided to take the direct route. So, splash, it dove in and swam across. And then, to shake the water off itself, it started doing a whole series of leaps and jumps! All of us birds laughed our heads off!"

"Then what?" the frogs ask.

"Then there was the departure of three young ducks; and the arrival of some teals, and then... and then..."

The moorhen goes on talking and talking for hours and hours. She is a real pond gossip!

28 Coots on the lake

Dozens and dozens of coots have gathered on the surface of the lake to rest. They sleep side by side, looking for all the world like lots of black feathers resting on a silvery mirror. They allow themselves to be rocked by the movement of the water, which lifts them all up and drops them down together.

The ducks keep away from them, since the coots don't have a very good reputation. They are agressive and quarrelsome birds. The ducks, though, are well aware that in a few days their black-suited guests will be leaving.

29 The badger's manners

Of course, being so big and clumsy, the badger has some poor manners. It enjoys sitting outside its den and scratching its thick fur with its big strong nails. At times it even lies on its back and massages its big tummy; and this is not exactly refined behavior, you must admit.

However, when it comes to eating nuts, the badger shows that it has very good table manners. It extracts the soft kernel from the shell and holds it daintily before putting it into its mouth!

30 The forgetful squirrel

What are all those agitated movements in the undergrowth? It is only a young squirrel who cannot find the hiding place in which is has stored its supplies for the winter! It has mislaid the walnuts, acorns, beans, and dry fruits, its precious supplies for the lean months.

But the squirrel does not give up. It looks under the roots of the pine tree, but there are no walnuts there. It rummages beneath the honeysuckle bush; not even a sign of a pine cone. It digs under a large, cracked rock, but there isn't a trace of an acorn. It picks through the clods of earth, but there isn't any fruit. It goes and looks down at the bottom of a moss-covered hole, but not a bean to be seen.

Then it grows angry and taps its paws on the ground in despair. Along comes the little squirrel's mother: "Don't get so excited; you'll see that when you least expect it you'll find your supplies. But let this be a lesson to you. You youngsters are always so absent-minded and lazy. When you put away your supplies, you have to take a very good look at the hiding place before you leave it. From now on, pay attention to your surroundings so that you can remember where you hide things."

31 The figure in the fog

As day breaks, a thick fog is hanging over the countryside. The hare strains its eyes as hard as possible, but all it can see is cotton wool white. It perks up its ears, but it can only hear muffled sounds. In spite of all this, it decides to go on a raiding expedition to the vegetable garden.

On its way, the vague outline of a large figure suddenly blocks its path. The little hare flees in terror! What a lot of panic for nothing! Because of the fog, it did not recognize the scarecrow that it sees every day.

1 Ripe pears for the wasps

In the orchard, the pale, autumn sunshine warms the pears, hanging in all their finery from the branches.

Of course, the sun is now weak; its rays no longer have the strength, the warmth or the brightness that they had at the height of the summer. But the warmth is still enough to complete the ripening of the pears and make them succulent and sweet.

The wasps appreciate this, because they know all about sweet things. They are the first to enjoy the pears!

2 The ladybug's winter house

There are no more cucumbers in the vegetable garden. James, the gardener, has picked them all. And there aren't any more of the aphids who were continually climbing up and down the stems of the vegetable plants. The first frost has wiped them out. But if there aren't any more aphids, what are the ladybugs going to eat from now on? Well, since ladybugs do not eat anything except aphids, they will not eat at all. Will they die of hunger?

No, they won't die. As soon as the aphids, their source of food, come to an end, all the ladybugs can do is to go into hibernation. Asleep and motionless, they will be able to survive without eating. Any movement would give them an appetite: especially the movements they make in summer, like running on all six legs along the stems of the roses, or launching themselves in risky flight from one branch of the apple tree to another.

For the long months to come, there will be no more outings and flights, but a lot of peace and rest. But first, they have to find a suitable resting place. And this is why the yellow ladybug, with six black dots on its back, chooses a secure wooden house. It slips into a crack in the trunk of a tree.

3 The red ladybug is particular

The fine, red ladybug, which has only two little black spots on its back, has chosen the dark blue velvet edge of the living room curtains, as the place to spend the winter months. It will make its home in the rich, soft material.

Because it is rather choosy, the ladybug had trouble finding somewhere it likes. There were other possible choices: satin, silk or wool. The decision was difficult to make, but in the end the velvet won, because it is soft and warm and, perhaps, because blue is a very peaceful color!

4 Autumn flowers

Laura's garden is all yellow, red, and orange. They are the warm colors typical of autumn, and during sunny days they take on golden reflections.

The sun comes up later every morning, and a persistent rain has been falling for the last few days, but the garden is still bright with the last of the flowers. There are giant dahlias with scarlet petals, and smaller dahlias with bright yellow petals. And there are violet-colored asters, adding even more variety to the display of colors.

5 The brown bear and the honeycomb

Up on the high mountain slopes, in the deep woods, the time has come for the little honeybees to put an end to their long summer's work. The good little bees have spent months sucking out the nectar from the thousands of little flowers spread in the high mountain meadows. During the summer, there was nothing but peace up there, but the calm hardworking bees had suffered a sudden catastrophe.

On a hot afternoon towards the end of the summer, they lost a large number of honeycombs, one after another. They had all been noisily destroyed.

Who had done the wicked deed?

The brown bear! It seems incredible, but up in these isolated woods there are still a few specimens of this animal. After having looked at the tree with the beehive on it, the bear had reared up on its hind legs and stuck its enormous paw into the crack in the trunk. The sentry bees reacted immediately. They chased him away by attacking his one weak point, the nose, and he barely had enough time to push a few honeycombs into his mouth.

Having chased off the attacker, the hard-working bees immediately began repairing the damage that the bear had done, and then started building up the reserves of honey again. But now that winter is at the door, the flowers are becoming rare and the days are growing shorter, and the bees are getting ready to take refuge in the hollow trunk for a well-earned rest! The bees in the chestnut tree, on the other hand, which is several hundred feet down, will move into their hive a bit later. This is almost a luxury hotel, if it is compared to the hive of their relatives up in the mountains. But, then, garden bees are delicate things, while those from the high mountains are more robust, and able to cope with the problems of living at high altitudes!

6 The fox in the storm

Suddenly, the clouds that were filling the sky seemed to explode. A torrential downpour struck the woods. At once, dense curtains of rain closed in over the trees, tearing off the last leaves that were still attached to them. The rain began to run down the bark of the trees, soaking the grass and the tender little plants in the undergrowth, flooding paths and trails.

It was almost a flood!

Under the canopy of the trees, you could hear a dull, continuous rumble. Sudden, furious downpours followed one after another. The rumble of thunder and the roar of the waterfall added their voices to that of the rain. The whole forest seemed to be playing the same magical tune.

The fox was caught by surprise in the sudden storm, and stopped in its tracks, annoyed by this violent shower. Looking to the right and then to the left, it spied a little cave under some big rocks, and in three quick bounds it reached safety there.

Well protected in its "hideout", the cunning fox has nothing else to worry about for the moment, and it slowly nods off to sleep.

7 The fox is hunting

On a fine, sunny afternoon, the fox puts its head out of the den. It sniffs the air all around, sticking out its pointed muzzle with the long whiskers. Its yellow eyes, narrowed down to slits, shine with determination. It yawns once, then again and "hop", out it goes. Time to go on a prowl.

It trots off along a small, stony path, covered by rustling, dry leaves. Then it passes under the half-naked trees, and enters the woods, beside a wide, peaceful field.

"Help, help!" yells a mouse, recognizing that long pointed muzzle instantly. "Help, help!" it repeats, diving down a hole as fast as it can.

Somewhat annoyed at seeing such an easy prey escape from under its nose, the fox continues on its way.

"Help, help!" yells a partridge this time, as it leaps out of a tuft of heather, and with a frightened squawk takes off in flight.

The fox angrily turns around and goes back into the woods.

"Help, help!" squeals a hare, when it sees it coming. This time the fox races after it.

Who is going to win this race?

8 The fox relocates

Do you like moving house? Do you like changing everything round, making a new home? Most of us do not really enjoy it, because of all the work.

As for the fox, he seems to love it. It would seem that he takes a delight in change and enjoys getting to know new places. But the fox is also a very prudent character. For example, he doesn't want you to know his address. If you discover his den, he moves at once! That is why the big red vixen is now going to live on the ground floor of the badger's house.

9 The unlucky vixen

Coming back empty-handed from her hunt, the vixen is depressed. Perhaps the moonlight made her too easy to spot? Perhaps the fieldmice and the countrymice had been alerted by the owl?

It is hard to say: usually she is so quick and cunning, this time she cannot figure out what went wrong.

And so, with a weary groan, the hungry vixen sets off again, but this time in the direction of the village.

The cunning mother fox knows of a certain, well-inhabited chicken coop, where all the hens are very well fed.

The vixen also knows that there is a hole in the fence, and that at night the dog sleeps, curled up down in the back of his house. She is already dreaming about the juicy meal awaiting her. But when she arrives at the fence, she finds, to her great disappointment, that the hole has been repaired. There can be no doubt that this really is an unlucky night for a vixen!

Meanwhile, she is growing so hungry that she is unable to think clearly. Her head is spinning and her eyesight grows hazy, while her legs begin to tremble. Feeling rather sick, the poor animal begins to groan and turns back towards her home.

10 The first ball game

Clank! Clink! Bonk!

The empty can bounces once, twice, three times on the path, against a stone, and then against a tree.

Three fox cubs examine this unusual object with a great deal of interest. They have never seen anything like it before. None of them dares touch it at first. Then the bravest of the three starts this new game, flipping the strange object with his muzzle. Clank! The noise of the tin bouncing on the path excites them, so much so that the cubs then settle down to their first game of ball!

11 Golden flowers from the East

James is preparing to hold a sale of seasonal plants. There are lots of lovely flowers which will brighten up grey, rainy days with their bright colors; from red to dark red, from yellow to golden yellow. These flowers have curved, tubular petals, so thickly inter-woven that they seem to form a sort of soft ball. They are very elegant flowers, and come originally from the East.

"What are they called?" asks a little admirer.

"Chrysanthemums," replies James.

It is a word which comes from Greek, and means "golden flowers".

12 The quiet woodpecker

I have actually seen a green woodpecker, which keeps silent! It doesn't sound possible, does it?

Everyone always thinks of the woodpecker as being a noisy neighbor, with that deafening pneumatic drill of his!

He is regarded as a troublemaker, both boring and repetitive since he plays the same "tune" from morning till night. In fact, with his endless tap-tap-tapping, he really disturbs the public peace.

And yet, I can assure you that the green woodpecker can also be silent. I discovered this while looking out of the window which overlooks the garden. The woodpecker was beside the lilac bush. I recognized it by its shiny, green feathers and its strong, well-developed beak.

It was calmly hopping on the tufts of grass, making regular stops, almost like a mechanical toy.

Its rhythmic movements didn't surprise me: they were typical of these birds. But what did surprise me was the fact that it kept quiet. From the open window, I could see it jumping and regularly pecking away at the damp earth, all in complete silence.

13 The woodpecker's worm hunt

Beside the big lilac bush, which no longer has the sweet-smelling bunches of flowers hanging from it, there is a carpet of soft moss, dotted with dozens and dozens of holes. Immediately, I think of that green woodpecker. It must have been him who made all those holes; to find the worms that he eats. That would also explain his constant leaping.

Underneath the clumps of grass, the worms mistake the rhythmic thudding of the bird's beak for falling rain, and out they come. Then, zip, the greedy woodpecker gobbles them up!

14 The thieving crow

Where is that shrill, persistent shrieking coming from?

Who has black and white feathers and a long tail with bluish reflections? Who is it? Why, it's the crow, of course! It is a bird which is famous for some very unusual reasons. Unlike many others, the crow is a bird which doesn't leave us when winter comes. Why doesn't it migrate? Because it is still able to find food even during the cold months. In fact, the crow doesn't just eat insects, larvae, and worms, which are the main food sources of other birds, it eats also pods and seeds. That is why it can always find something to eat. And so the crow always stays here with us, brightening up the trees and bushes in our parks even when they are bare of leaves.

The crow also has another very unique characteristic: it is a notorious thief! And what do you think it steals — almost anything bright, colorful, or sparkling. It seems to be attracted to anything that shines: colored stones, rings, pins, bracelets, and necklaces: anything as long as it shines.

So be very careful when you see a crow... it might be planning to steal something precious from you!

15 Pudding and the apples

Today is a lovely day, cool and dry. Emily takes advantage of it to finish picking the apples. Mark and Clare have offered to help her. Pudding, Clare's cat, has followed them into the orchard.

Pudding is in a very lively mood today, and is soon being told to stop its mischief.

To begin with, it climbs up the ladder, and Emily nearly stands on its tail on her way down. You can imagine the chaos if that had happened! Not content with that, Pudding jumps onto the pile of boxes for packing the fruit. The whole pile begins to sway, and then it all tumbles over on top of the cat, which ends up lying on the grass beneath a heap of boxes.

At that point, Pudding decides it is best to move away from the scene of the disaster, and goes to the bottom of the orchard to see what is going on there.

But when calm returns, so too does Pudding, as if nothing has happened. The cat lies down and goes to sleep in the cart beside Mark.

16 The apple harvest storehouse

Mark and Clare go with Emily to look at the harvested apples.

"What a lovely smell," says Clare, sniffing the air.

The delicate perfume seems to fill the whole room where the apples are kept in the cool semi-darkness.

"But I can hardly see anything!" protests Clare. Only a small amount of light filters through a narrow window. "Why is there so little light?" she asks, in surprise.

"The apples keep better in the dark: in a dim, cool place they last for longer. You have to leave them to rest," explains Emily. "These pallets piled one on top of the other, make a comfortable bed for the apples, a kind of bunk bed."

"And will you leave your apples here forever?" asks Mark. "We will come and check up on them from time to time. We'll move them around a bit, and turn them over to see if any are going bad. You have to be very careful: if an apple goes bad in just one spot, or grows some mold, then in no time at all the ones around it go bad also."

"Apple molds are contagious. But we make sure we choose the nicest looking apples to eat for dinner throughout the winter."

17 Things to do with apples

Today's science lesson was all about the apple. With the help of large, color illustrations, everyone was able to see how an apple is formed and develops, from the flower to the fruit.

Then the lesson became more light-hearted and they spoke of the many qualities of apples, which, apart from being delicious, are also very good for your health.

"Do you know anything you can make with apples?" asks the teacher.

The answers come at him from all over the classroom.

"One at a time!" says the teacher.

With their eyes shining, all the children seem to have ideas on this subject. Everyone is interested where apples are concerned.

"You can make apple pie!"

"Apple jam!"

"Baked apples!"

"You can make cider," says another little boy.

"You can core them and cook them with jam in the center."

"Enough, enough! It sounds like the dessert menu in a restaurant!" exclaims the teacher.

One thing is for sure, while it might not be as exotic as some other fruits, the apple is one of the most popular and varied in its uses.

18 The hedgehog's winter bed

The hedgehog walks across the garden, thinking: "Isn't it cold? It is time to get my bed ready for the winter!"

The hedgehog begins to search systematically for dry leaves, which it then drags back to its den.

It trots back and forth and builds up a nice, big pile of dry, soft birch leaves, mixed with grass and flower stems. Eventually it will lie down on this mattress, and roll from side to side, making a nice, round hollow for itself.

19 A weak, pale sun

Much to his surprise, Matthew discovered that, in winter, the sun not only rises late, but it is in a different part of the sky than in the summer. During the summer, when it shone through the shutters at eight in the morning, he saw the huge luminous disc right above the chestnut tree.

Now, when he opens his shutters at eight o'clock, there is no sign of the sun, in fact it is still dark, and Matthew wants to go back to bed. What a change from the summer when the sun and the birds awakened him in the morning!

When Matthew gets up an hour later, on Sundays, he finds that the sun has then risen, but it is not in the same position as it was during the summer. It just peeks over the small walnut tree. And it doesn't shine so brightly either. Instead it appears pale and weak. As if this wasn't enough, the fog also lends a hand in making it less bright. Not to mention the fact that the sun sometimes stays hidden for days on end behind a thick blanket of cloud. Then its rays have little warmth and its light is dull.

Matthew doesn't like the look of that sickly sun. "It's the autumn sun," sighs his mother. "We just have to put up with it."

20 The hedgehog and the farm dog

The hedgehog has decided to pad the nest it is preparing for its winter den very thoroughly. For this reason, it is continually going back and forth carrying bundles of leaves. During one of its trips, however, it finds itself face to face with a farm dog. As soon as it sees the dog, the hedgehog rolls into a ball.

The dog moves around and around the little ball of quills, and decides that this moving cactus is not for him! Better get moving: his nose might get hurt!

21 So many mushrooms

Thanks to the rain and the high humidity, lots of mushrooms have grown in the woods.

Mushrooms don't have roots, or a stem, or leaves, and they come in a wide variety of shapes. Most of the time they have a large head, on top of a long or a swollen stalk, but some even look like trumpets. And they come in all colors: yellow, white, brown, red, black...

Whether eaten raw or cooked, certain mushrooms are really delicious. But watch out! Many of them, often the nicest looking ones, are poisonous.

22 When a hedgehog meets a viper

The hedgehog is out for another walk, but today he meets along the path not the farm dog, but a viper!

Because it is perfectly protected against a snake's bite, the hedgehog isn't afraid of the viper, as we are. When it comes face to face with its old enemy, the hedgehog, usually so calm and mild, must use its natural defenses, and summon up all its fighting reserves. And so the hedgehog gives up its walk, stops thinking about gathering leaves for its winter shelter, and prepares for combat.

First, it prepares its weapons: it lowers a kind of spiky visor over it forehead, and it protects its flanks, which are its most vulnerable part, by extending other formidable quills.

Faced with such a heavily armed and determined warrior, the viper has no chance, and it slithers away as fast as it can. It is just as well, because the hedgehog would certainly have won the battle. That is why the harmless little hedgehog is so valued in the garden when there are vipers around.

23 An autumn night's feast

It is not true that all the autumn nights are cold. Sometimes they are still quite warm, and all the hedgehogs take advantage of these to organize parties in the woods or in the vegetable garden.

They have a large assortment of snacks to choose from. They can start with a nice apple to whet the appetite; then a few, wild plums, since they are nearly finished; followed by a helping of mushrooms, at their best at this time. Acorns and beans, that crunch under their teeth, round off the meal. A real feast, on a warm, soft, autumn night!

24 The visions in the mist

Andrew is staying with his Aunt Maggie for the weekend. This morning he is awake very early, just after dawn, because he is anxious to begin his day exploring.

He opens the shutters very quietly, not to wake anyone up. His eyes are greeted by an unusual sight. The garden is wrapped in a soft, white mist. Through the fog, Andrew can see the river flowing and, beyond it, the grove of fruit trees, where the wild apple trees, which have already lost almost all their leaves, still have some stunted apples on them.

The trees along the riverbank loom out of the mist like a row of giants. There is a smell of damp earth in the air, and everything is quiet. Andrew's attention is caught by a slight rustling sound. At the edge of the woods, a doe and her fawn have appeared, as if by magic. They take a few steps towards the fruit grove and, cautiously, they enter it. The doe chews at some of the lower branches, then almost at once, runs off, followed by her young fawn. They disappear into the mist.

Andrew is full of wonder. Was it real or did he dream it?

25 The half-asleep hedgehog

After a series of windy days, the temperature has dropped considerably, and at last the hedgehog decides it is time to retire into its shelter, underneath the woodpile. There, it sinks into its soft bed of dry leaves, rolls around, curls up, stretches, curls up again and then rolls onto its side, at last finding the right position. Then it grunts and sneezes before finally calming down and dropping off to sleep.

For as long as the temperature is cold, but not really freezing, the hedgehog stays only half-asleep, and it hears noises coming from outside; the grinding of the teeth of a mouse as it chews something in the garden; the squeaking wheel of the wheelbarrow; a pine cone which falls onto the pile of wood overhead.

The poor hedgehog finds it very hard to get to sleep properly with all these disturbances going on around him!

26 Pumpkins of all shapes and sizes

It is the time of the pumpkins. Protected by their large rough-edged leaves, between creeping stalks and large flowers, the pumpkins, in all their various shapes, have ripened in the vegetable garden. There are "short-necked" pumpkins, and "turban-shaped" pumpkins. Then there are the "pilgrims" pumpkins, so-called because they look like pilgrims' sacks, and there are "violin-shaped" pumpkins. All these pumpkins can be made into water jugs, or pies, or, as in the fairy tale, a coach for Cinderella!

27 The prudent hare

Early in the morning, there is always a thin veil of mist hanging over the fields. Here and there, groups of trees stand out; you can barely see them with the forest behind.

As soon as it leaves its hiding place, the hare sniffs the damp air and recognizes a lot of familiar smells: the smell of smoke coming from the chimneys of the village nearby; the smell of the mushrooms in the woods; and the lovely smell of the recently plowed earth. It perks up its long ears and hears a lot of familiar sounds as well: in the distance, it can make out the engine of a tractor; and the constant grinding sound can only be the wheel of the mill turning. Other sounds reach it from down in the valley. It can hear the familiar dog barking; the one guarding the best vegetable patch in the district!

When it has identified all these sounds, the hare knows it is safe to cross the fields. Then, suddenly, the air is shattered by two loud shots and the sound of barking echoes around the fields. The hare doesn't know the cause of all this noise, but its instincts warn it of danger. In an instant, it turns and flees.

28 The hare's funny exercises

Outside the entrance to its burrow, the hare often performs an odd, gymnastic show. It stands up to its full height on its back legs, and, with its front paws, it bangs on its stomach, as if on a drum.

Perched up in the branches, some robins really enjoy this spectacle. "Ah, there goes our friend the hare, putting on his show again!" they chirp to each other. It is strange but true, that the hare often repeats this funny behavior when it comes home.

29 Saved by a clever trick

The hare hears that unknown, continuous barking again. This time it also spots a hunting dog which is obviously on its scent. The dog has lively eyes, a lolling tongue, and strong legs to leap over any obstacles on the ground.

The only way the hare can escape, is by using its cunning. At the very moment that the dog is about to leap on it, the hare, with a deft swerve, thwarts its attacker. It does an about-face and leaps past the dog, back in the direction it came from... and heads for safety!

30 As fast as a hare!

"My bicycle's got a flat tire!" says Clare.

"Get the pump and pump it up!" replies Mark. "It's not difficult!"

"It is for me. would you do it, please?" asks Clare.

"Oh, OK," Mark agrees, pretending to be annoyed. He really doesn't mind doing it. Clare is not very good at jobs like that!

Five minutes later, the two bicycles are ready to go. Mark and Clare ride along the paved road which winds between the two newly-plowed fields.

Suddenly, Clare shouts: "Look, look!, A hare!"

"Where?" says Mark. "I can't see it. Where is it?"

"Look, there it is, on the right hand side of that big furrow! Look, now there are two of them! Aren't they lovely!" Clare gets off her bicycle to take a better look.

Mark stops as well and narrows his eyes to focus on them better. It is hard to spot a hare, because their brown coats blend in with the brown color of the clumps of earth in the fields. Eventually, Mark sees the two hares bounding along the straight furrow.

"I can see three now!" shouts Mark in excitement.

"Yes, yes! I can see them too," yells Clare, clapping her hands.

"Let's follow along the road at the edge of the field on our bikes!" suggests Mark.

The two children ride away, pedaling as hard as they can. For a while they manage to keep them in sight, but as they approach the end of the field there is not a trace of the hares to be seen.

"But they were there, I saw them!" says Clare sadly.

"Yes, but hares are very fast!" says Mark with resignation.

1 The hare with the varying coat

With its round muzzle, its straight, short ears, full cheeks, and dark, lively eyes, it is easy to recognize the hare. It is called the mountain or varying hare. Recently it has changed a lot.

Its fur, which during the summer was brown, has now become very pale, almost white. Perhaps it has fallen into a bag of flour! Or maybe it has been sprayed with vanilla icing! Joking aside, its hair has become lighter in color throughout the autumn in anticipation of the change in the landscape, which will soon become white in the winter.

2 The salmon are returning

Over the last few days, there has been a lot of strange splashing going on in the raging mountain stream. Today, as fast as a flash of lightning, out of the spray there appears a huge, silvery salmon. With a mighty leap, it jumps over a rock, which projects above the raging river, and lands further upstream, disappearing into a white froth.

It is a salmon returning from its long journey, an adult salmon returning to the stream where it was born, at the end of a voyage across the sea which has lasted several years.

Just think about it: when it was still young, the brave fish swam down the bubbling stream where it was born. It swam through the raging waters, slipping down many waterfalls and long rapids, until finally it arrived in the calmer current of the great river. From there, swimming strongly, it reached the sea. Here it discovered salt water, and the ocean currents, a wonderful source of food, like crabs and shrimps, and off it went west across the ocean, following routes known only to the salmon.

3 Lords of the high peaks

A sheer rock face towers over a wild, mountain lake. The mountain is absolutely calm, but some dots are moving high up on the summit.

I focus my binoculars and can see a whole herd of chamois, calmly grazing on the mountainside. It looks impossible for them not to fall off the mountainside; they certainly do not seem to have any fear of heights!

Up on the high peaks, these lords of the mountain move around on the most sheer slopes, without difficulty.

4 The wild boar and the beets

The wild boar has very sure instincts, and a very healthy appetite. That is why it is always capable of finding the places where its favorite food is growing.

When autumn arrives, the wild boar goes to dig up the seasonal specialities. One of these has such a large, fleshy root, and such a sweet flavor, that the boar shivers in ecstacy when eating it. The unfortunate farmer who is growing a crop of beets will find large numbers of them gobbled up by the big, greedy boar!

5 Deer galloping past

The house in the mountains, belonging to Clare's grandparents, is surrounded by a big lawn, bordered by tall pine trees.

"When I was young," her grandfather tells her, "these trees were only the size of Christmas trees."

"And was it you who planted them?" asks Clare.

"Well, really it was my father. But my brothers and I helped him!" says her grandfather. "Come on now, it's time to go back into the house!"

Clare goes for a last walk around the meadow with her dolls' carriage. It is only four o'clock in the afternoon and it is already getting dark. It is cold and night will soon be falling. Then it will be nice to be in the house, with the fire burning.

Clare lingers a little longer with her thoughts. Everything is so calm. But then she hears a sudden noise: the ground vibrates, the air is filled with grunts, snorts and mighty sneezes. There is the unmistakable sound of an animal approaching at the gallop.

Clare runs over to the fence near the pine trees; and right beside her is a huge deer racing past like a steam engine. The animal gallops on, raising clods of earth, grass, and moss, and then disappears into the forest.

Clare remains beside the fence. Her heart is beating fiercely. A few moments later, the ground begins to tremble again. Then another deer, smaller than the first, gallops up and stops in its tracks a few feet away from the little girl. The animal hesitates, then takes a few steps towards the fence; then with a sudden bound, it changes direction, sets off at a gallop again, and disappears.

Clare can just make it out as it vanishes in long, elegant bounds into the dark. It is cold, but Clare doesn't notice. Her heart is still beating very fast because of all the excitement.

6 The badger's tenant

The fox with the long, flowing, red tail has a fine place to live. To be honest, it did not dig out its magnificent den by itself, because it was first built by the badger.

In a certain sense, the fox is merely a tenant, occupying one of the apartments in a large building. The badger has built himself a very large home, hidden under a chestnut tree trunk, all covered with moss and blackberries.

Inside, the solitary badger built himself lots of tunnels, on different levels, all linked up to each other by wells. The rooms where it lives are large and spacious, with high ceilings. The ones that it has rented to the fox are also very spacious, but are situated just a little below ground level. This is an excellent position for the intelligent fox to use as an observation post. From there it can keep an eye on everything that goes on all around.

Moreover, the fox has a cabinet in which it keeps prizes from its hunting trips.

So as not to disturb each other, the fox and the badger have agreed to go out at different times. It seems like a good arrangement.

7 The hedgehog goes out

After a few decidedly cold days and some decidedly freezing nights, the temperature has become more mild. The wind has dropped, the clouds have dispersed and the air has become surprisingly warm: it doesn't feel as if the winter is about to start.

In the warmth of its den, where it has been dozing for several days, the hedgehog has noticed this change. It awakens completely, moves its muzzle out from where it was tucked away, sniffs the air, shakes itself and, between one grunt and another, thinks: "I must be silly to stay in bed in this weather!"

So it pushes away its cover of leaves, rises from its bed and prepares to go out. What a lovely feeling it is, to stretch its legs again, to straighten out its quills, and take deep breaths of the fresh air in the garden! The hedgehog is feeling so good that it climbs the wall of the vegetable garden without pausing: it is an excellent opportunity to stretch its limbs.

And do you know how it gets back down? No problem at all! It simply curls up into a ball, and... one, two, three... it just lets itself roll off the wall!

8 The country mouse takes to the air!

The poor, little, country mouse has just undergone one terrible experience, and now it fears another one!

It was running along a fresh furrow in the newly-plowed field, when it suddenly realized that it was being followed. It had hardly caught sight of the fox when it was flung into the air by a flip of its muzzle.

The unlucky, little, country mouse expected to be caught, but instead, the fox just left without touching it again.

9 The beavers' floating storehouse

The winter is coming. The beavers can feel it. They know that they have to build up their supplies for the hard days to come.

They are such hard workers. They double up their shifts, and every night they go out to cut the branches of some trees along the river bank. With their sharp teeth, they saw off the branches of willow, poplar, and birch trees, and then chop them up. When they have done this, the beavers take all the branches back along special paths which they use as slides. Then they push them into the water of their canals and float them down as far as their lodge. There they begin a very delicate task. These extraordinary creatures join all the branches very skilfully, without wasting even one. They weave them and bind them, linking them so tightly that they will not come apart. This is not easy. Even for the busy beaver, it is a very tiring job.

But, in the end, they have made a perfect raft. It is a floating storehouse, which will help them to face the hardships of the coming winter.

10 The beaver that loves cabbages

There is one little beaver who is really unique. Of course, he is a hard worker, just like all his companions. He chops down trees; he cuts up branches; he sails the wood down the river; he takes part in the building of dams and lodges; he swims and dives into the water continually, along with all the rest.

But sometimes, during the day, instead of taking a nap like the others, he prefers to go out of the lodge and swim over to the nearby vegetable patch, where there are some lovely cabbages growing.

The beaver adores them... and it devours them greedily!

11 The salmon returns to its birthplace

A large salmon has just returned to the river in which it was born. During the long time it was away at sea, it ate lovely shrimps, crunchy crabs, hundreds of tiny fish, and it has grown into an enormous adult salmon, over three feet long. A wonderful specimen!

His stay in the estuaries and the open sea has caused him to develop strong jaws, elongated and hooked, but it has also dulled his shiny coat a little. These are the signs that he is now of a mature age.

12 Why the salmon has returned

The young salmon swim around their new guest. They examine this new member of the family with curiosity, noticing that it doesn't resemble any of them, and for this reason they keep a respectful distance.

There is no doubt that it is different. Not only is it much bigger than they are, but even the color of its skin is different. It is more or less grey with no blue reflections, and its mouth has grown into the shape of a large hook. But it is not so much its exterior which makes it different from the other salmon, as its character. This shows that it must have lived far from home for a very long time. It has other tastes, other habits. For example, ever since it swam up the river it hasn't eaten a thing; it refuses all types of food!

"Well then, why did it come back?" the young salmon wonders. "Why didn't it stay out in the ocean?"

"It has come back to start a family," someone says. A female salmon will lay its eggs in the same place where it was born."

That is why the big salmon has come back home again!

13 The long, dangerous journey

It is a very dangerous and exhausting journey for a salmon to make to return to the stream where it was born. Upon leaving the ocean, it stays for a while in the estuary of a river to get used to fresh water again. Then it begins to swim up the river. But how does it manage to find its "own" river? Its very sharp sense of smell allows it to recognize the odors and scents of its "own" water.

The journey up river is full of perils. The salmon has to beware of fishermen, and overcome barriers and waterfalls, with courage and determination, as it swims up the river.

14 A valuable tail!

The beaver beats its tail rhythmically as it swims along the edge of the river. What an amazing tail it has! Oval-shaped, large and flat, partially covered by hairs, and in part by small, brown scales, it is incredibly versatile and of immense value to the beaver.

Besides being used as an engine and a rudder, the beaver's flat tail also helps it to keep its balance much of the time. While doing certain jobs, the beaver is able to lean on it for support, or by holding it straight up, it manages to stay perfectly balanced. When it is in the water, busy building a raft, for instance, the beaver beats its tail continually, managing in this way to float without having to swim.

It is a first-class rudder. When the beaver is swimming, it can change direction when it pleases, with a flick of its tail to the left or to the right. And to add to all this, this wonderful tail functions as an excellent danger-warning device. If the beaver beats its tail very hard and dives under the water, the splashing of the water and the spray cause a general, red alert all around.

15 Maintaining the lodge

The beavers' lodge has a reputation for being a very solid, safe, and comfortable construction. But what a lot of maintenance work it requires!

The hard-working little beavers check it all the time to make sure it is secure, discover any cracks and look for any signs of sinking. And as soon as it is necessary, they begin repairing it. That is how they maintain their reputation as skilful builders.

Their ability becomes even more important as the winter approaches. The beavers begin their renovation in plenty of time, so that the lodge will resist the persistent cold, the driving rain, and the repeated snow storms of the winter. As snow builds up on the roof, it has to be very strong to hold up under the weight of the white blanket.

So, as soon as it starts to get cold, the beavers concentrate their efforts on strengthening the roof. Then they dig up small amounts of mud from the bottom of the river, and with their paws they press it into all the cracks. When it dries out, the mud becomes very hard and it will keep their house strong, dry and weather-proof.

16 The first snowfall

Perched at the top of a poplar tree, a raven croaks to the four winds. Its harsh, tuneless call pierces the ear.

The tireless raven never stops croaking: "The winter is coming! The winter is coming! Beware! Beware!"

And the raven is right. Because out of the dull grey sky come thousands of small snowflakes, swirling and dancing their way to the ground.

It is the first snowfall of the winter.

17 The hunting of the hare

Once again, the fox has surprised the hare outside its burrow, and chases it immediately. "Whatever it costs," says the fox, "today I want to catch that fellow with the long ears! Last time he escaped from right underneath my nose!"

The fox chases... and the hare flees. One after the other, the two animals cross a wide stretch of land, where a patchy covering of blades of newly-sown wheat is already showing through.

With its ears lowered onto its back, the hare flees desperately, leaping on its long, furry legs, as if they were strong springs. It runs quickly!

"What can I do to escape?" the hare asks itself. It tries a sudden swerve to one side. It enters a furrow. It races off again in the opposite direction. It runs faster and faster in its attempt to escape.

The freezing air blows across the muzzle of the hare. The fox is almost close behind.

The desperate chase lasts for a long time. At one point, it seems as if the fox is about to trap its prey with its paw, but once again it escapes.

"It is time to use my brain, if my legs aren't sufficient!" thinks the fox. He devises a plan. The fox slows down and calls for help from another fox. There must be one somewhere in the area. Another fox hears the cry and settles down to lie in wait in a spot that the hare will be forced to pass sooner or later.

Now the fox takes up the chase again with more confidence. It is simple: all he has to do is chase the hare to where his ally is hiding! Who is going to win this time, the hare or the fox?

18 The hare takes a rest

The hare has changed its burrow again. It has moved in under a bush at the edge of the clearing.

It is exhausted after its escape the day before, and for some time it doesn't move from its hiding place. It is resting and listening. It isn't easy to get over that wild chase. It only just managed to get away from that second fox which jumped out on it suddenly. The hare managed to get away, to cover its tracks and get to safety in its new home.

19 The foxes try to forget

"What bad luck! What a disgrace! How humiliating! We had that hare in our paws and it managed to get away!" The two frustrated foxes are very unhappy at not having been able to catch the hare.

They continue to let out yelps of misery for a long time. But, in the end, they go back into the forest.

It is cold. The wind whistles through the naked branches. The sky is leaden grey, swollen with snow. A slight sleet is already falling. Tiny slivers of ice fly through the air, carried by the wind.

The two foxes climb up a slight slope. They are agile, fast, and light. When they reach the top, they go down the other side silently. Then they move into a grove of tall trees.

Long, cut trunks lie piled up on the thick layer of dead leaves. With easy agility, the two foxes jump onto the wood. There, they play at chasing each other and keeping their balance, probably just to pass the time until something better comes along. They forget all about the hare. The foxes are happy again. They play like two gymnasts on the exercise beam!

20 Snow all around

The garden is bare and cold, but Skip the fox terrier is sleeping happily in his comfortable, green-painted house. He has enjoyed his meal: a hearty soup that filled him up, warmed him, and made him feel sleepy.

"With this grey sky, all I can do is go to sleep," Skip thinks to himself. But when he wakes up a few hours later, Skip thinks he is still dreaming. "It's all white!" he barks joyfully. Large, white snowflakes are still falling from the sky.

Autumn means heavy bunches of grapes, yellow and purple.
The season also brings crunchy, red and yellow apples, golden
pears that melt in your mouth... and a few scratches to show
after climbing the trees in an attempt to get at the ripest fruits.

Grapes

Figs

The autumn is a feast of delicious fruits which hold the heat and the light of the sun in their pulp, together with the sweet taste of the summer.

Autumn is the time for harvesting and storing. The barns are filled, and roofs are repaired so as to be ready for the cold season which is coming.

The woodchucks are busy gathering in dry grass to make their den soft and warm for the winter.

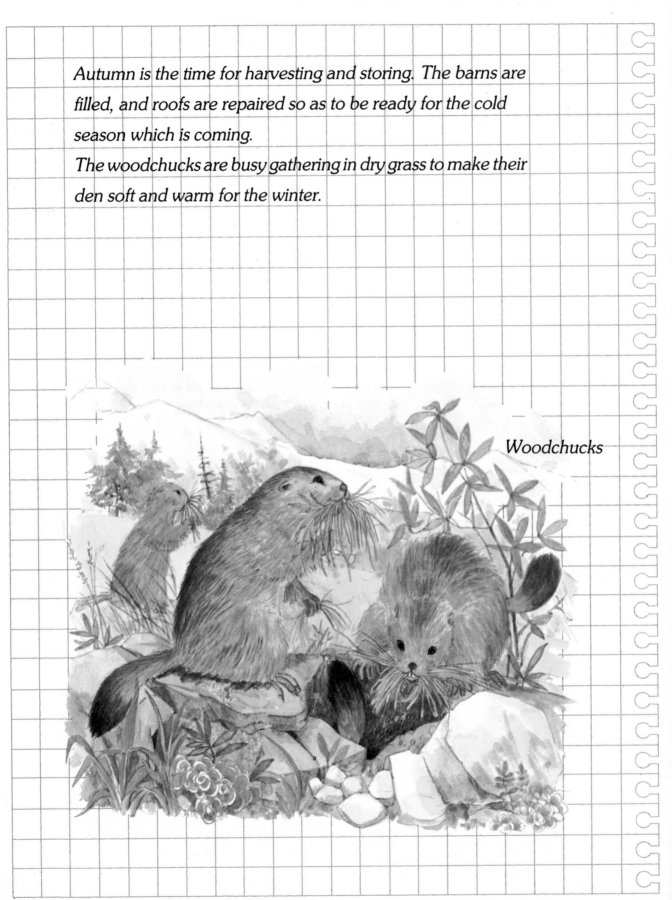

Woodchucks

The autumn is also the time for long journeys. Many birds fly off to distant lands, to look for warmer weather. Ducks and swallows all gather together in groups and fly off towards the south.

Wild Ducks

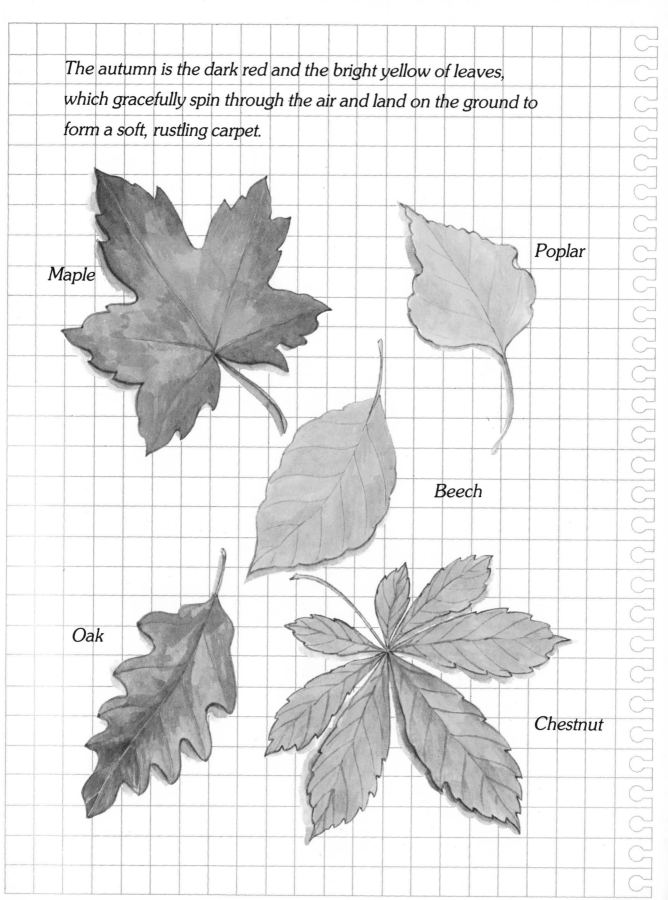

The autumn is the dark red and the bright yellow of leaves, which gracefully spin through the air and land on the ground to form a soft, rustling carpet.

Maple

Poplar

Beech

Oak

Chestnut

Autumn is also the season in which thousands of strange, odd shapes appear in the woods, with large, brown, red, or yellow tops. They are the mushrooms and toadstools, which spring up among the roots of the old trees and on the green mosses after a day of rain.

The autumn brings the last flowers before the cold, damp fogs take over. In the garden, dahlias and astors are out; the rich colors of the chrysanthemums brighten the flower beds. A bunch of all these flowers is as cheerful as a firework display.

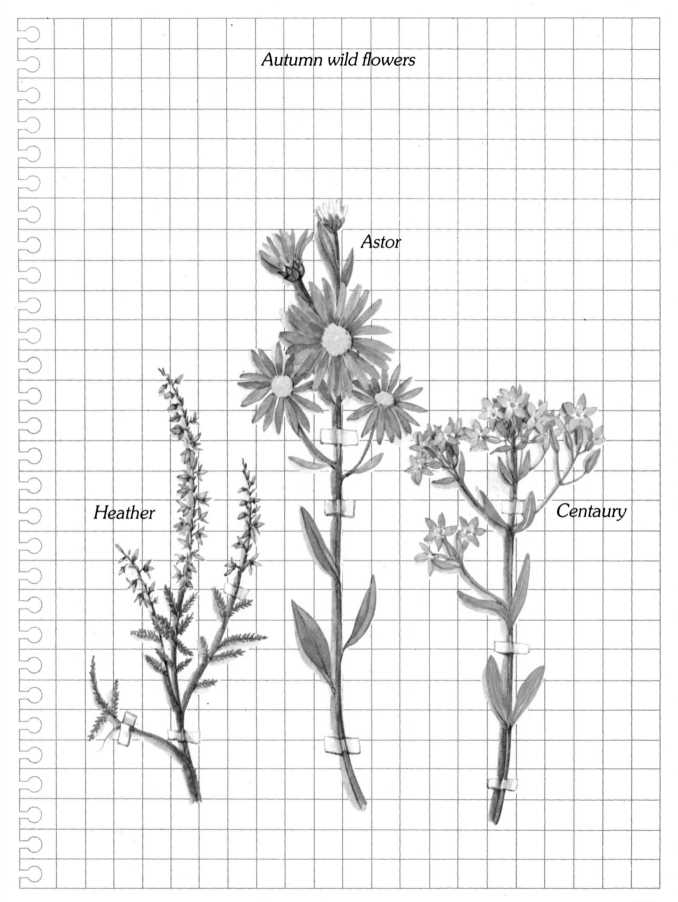

Autumn wild flowers

Astor

Heather

Centaury

Contents

A mouse in a drawer

The Smith family has decided to rent a house in the country. They plan to go there every weekend and for holidays with their children, Paula and Alexander, aged ten and eight, respectively.

The Smiths are city dwellers and it is because they live there, amid smog and noise, that they love the countryside so much. The mother and father have always wanted to live in the country. They fell in love with the house they are now renting on their first visit. It is an old, country building, very pretty and homey, with rustic furniture, big beds and an enormous kitchen which makes you want to prepare wholesome, traditional dishes.

Then there is the garden! And beyond the garden, the park! And beyond the park is the open country! There are so many wonderful places for walks.

"This summer I am going to learn the names of the wildflowers in the fields," says Paula.

"And I plan to build a wooden hut in the meadow," Alexander states.

"Won't it be nice to plant some roses!" adds their mother.

"As for me, I'm going to sit outside in the evenings in the cool air and play my guitar," says their father, quite elated at the thought.

"What a pity we still have to wait for so long. We have to get through the winter first," he continues.

"But we will still have some lovely weekends. We will go for long walks and enjoy the peace and quiet of the country."

It seems ages before the first weekend that they are going to spend in the country arrives. They all help in the packing, and are all caught up in the spirit of things. In the end, there is so much luggage that father protests, even though he was the one who turned up at the last moment with an accordion and a guitar!

Moving into the new house does not go smoothly!

"It's freezing!" exclaims their mother, in disappointment. "Of course! The radiators are cold. We have to turn the central heating on at once."

Dad stops unloading the luggage and begins turning the knobs on the boiler. It is not easy and the boiler refuses to light. They all have to go to bed early on their first night, after having piled on lots of extra blankets.

The next day, Saturday, it is raining and that gives them time to organize the house and solve the problem of the boiler. They succeed with the help of Peter, a farmer who lives nearby.

"There's a great, big spider's web here!" shouts Paula, always excited

when she spots one. But no one pays attention to her!

"There are all sorts of things in these drawers, from buttons to brooches," complains their mother, who is sorting out the clothes. "Who knows if they have been cleaned out in the last twenty years!" Sighing, she goes off to get a duster.

There is a wooden staircase, which is finely polished and waxed, but, unfortunately, every step creaks, especially during the night. These noises make them all a little uneasy.

However, the pleasant surprises greatly outnumber the minor inconveniences, except for the creaking of the stairs, which everyone gradually gets used to.

On Sunday morning, the sky is clear blue and the air is sharp, making everyone feel very energetic. They are all in high spirits. After having breakfast in the big kitchen, the children dash out into the garden, followed by their parents, ready for a healthy walk in the park.

Over the following weeks, in spite of the cold and the snow which makes the roads very difficult to drive on, the family goes back to their house in the country if not every weekend, at least every two weeks. By now, father knows exactly how the boiler works, and also knows how to make a great wood fire in the big fireplace. At times,

when it is very cold, they prefer to spend the afternoon reading or playing music beside the fire, rather than going for a walk.

They are all in love with country life, and the big house now holds no more secrets for them. But, are there really any big houses without secrets?

One evening, before going to bed, mother goes to get a large woollen shawl out of a drawer. She unfolds it, only to find that there is a large hole right through it from top to bottom.

"How did that happen?" she wonders. It isn't until the next day that Theresa, Peter's wife, can provide any explanation for this mystery.

"It is a dormouse, there's no doubt about it," declares Theresa, assuredly.

"A dormouse? You mean that lovely, little mouse with the sharp, pointed nose and the long, furry tail?" asks Paula. "But I thought they went into hibernation in a den in the woods?"

"Usually they do, but it wouldn't be the first time that a dormouse had sneaked into the furniture, and dug a nice nest out of all the softest pieces of clothing it could find."

"A dormouse in the drawer!" exclaims Paula, laughing. But when she goes to look for it, the cunning, little animal has already moved somewhere else!

21 In the fir forest

Today, the woodsmen have gone into the forest. One by one, they look at the fir trees, making a white mark on the ones which are growing too close together, or else do not have many branches, or have some other defect.

Later on, they return with long saws and begin cutting into the bark of the trees they had marked.

Throughout the afternoon, the shrill sound of the saws echoes through the woods. Then, in the evening, the chopped-down fir trees are loaded on to a truck and taken away. Silence once again falls on the forest.

22 Choosing a tree

In the markets and on the street corners of the cities, lots of fir trees, both large and small, have begun to appear. Some are long and slender, and others are short and fat, with bent tops.

Mothers and fathers with their children wander among these trees, trying to decide which one to take.

These fir trees come from cold forests far away, and still retain a strong smell of resin. Their long, flexible branches are covered with thin, bright green needles.

It is an important choice to have to make. The fir tree is going to be the center of attention. So many happy eyes will be drawn to it. All the children, of course, want a big Christmas tree. "I want it to reach up to the roof!" shouts a little girl, pointing out an enormous one. Her mother thinks of the space she has and decides that the tree can't be too big. Sometimes there is only enough space for a small one to put on the living room table.

The adults with tastes similar to the children are the dads! They also want big Christmas trees to put in the middle of the living room.

23 The mice in the attic

As soon as the door to the attic squeaks open and the shadows of the two children spread across the floor, the two little mice take off as fast as their legs will carry them.

What a shame! They were having such a good time in the big attic, which is covered by a fine grey dust and decorated with giant cobwebs. The mice could wander at their leisure among old trunks, cardboard boxes and piled up chairs.

"The Christmas decorations are in that yellow box," says Clare to her brother. "I hope we don't find any mice in among them... You open it!"

24 Nature's gift for Christmas

In their aunt's house, by the old mill, the preparations for the Christmas festivities are almost complete. Joan and Andrew have helped her a lot, not just with suggestions, but also by hanging the decorations from the branches of the tree, and above the doors and windows.

Joan found a roll of red ribbon in one of her aunt's baskets. She tied the ribbon to the lower branches of the fir tree. The result is a perfect Christmas decoration.

The tree is ready. It is a good shape and just the right size. Now it is all decorated with multi-colored, shiny baubles, with chocolates wrapped in silver paper, and with gold and silver tinsel hanging down from the upper branches.

"It is magnificent! Really magnificent!" exclaims their aunt. "But something is missing: something very important, in fact, indispensable. The holly is missing. That is what Nature gives us as a present for Christmas. If you go out into the woods, you will find some. It is the only green plant among all the other brown ones."

For Christmas dinner, the bright red berries of the green holly add the final touch to the beauty of the dining room.

25 Good luck for Christmas

The unusual heat spreading through the big living room slowly rises up to the ceiling, and ends up waking the ladybug out of its winter sleep, where it was nestling in between the folds of the velvet curtains. Feeling new energy, the ladybug shakes off the effects of its long sleep, and slowly begins moving along the soft material; then it takes a look around. What a splendid sight it sees down below. The big living room is all decked out for the occasion. Today, there will be a big feast.

A bright fire is burning in the stone fireplace, throwing out lots of sparks all around. The lamps spread their light through the room. A huge fir tree, loaded with decorations and presents, makes the scene even more joyful.

The exchanging of presents begins, and the room is filled with exclamations of joy and surprise.

At that point, the ladybug decides that it wants to take part in the general fun as well. It spreads its wings, takes off and flies through the air... and lands on the hand of a pretty girl.

"Luck has landed on you today!" everyone exclaims at once. "Ladybugs are always bearers of good luck!"

26 The guinea pig

"A wooden box? I wonder what's in it," says Mark, going up to the tree which is surrounded by presents, each with a name clearly written on it. Before opening the strange box, he hesitates a moment and then decides to lift the lid. On a bed of hay is lying a guinea pig, the nicest-looking one that Mark has ever seen!

It has brown, black and white fur, lively eyes, and a cute, little face. The little mammal seems anything but asleep. In fact, it is ready to go nosing about in every direction.

27 A pair of canaries

An unusual chirping can be heard through the living room door. In the middle of winter, even if there are woods nearby, it is rather unusual. The chirping is constant and varied. At times it is melodious, like a musical instrument, at others, it is shrill or staccato. Go and take a look!

There are two canaries, one bright yellow and the other a lovely, orange color, flying around in a big cage, their singing filling the whole room. Joan has been given them as a present from her aunt.

"Thank you, thank you so much!"

exclaims Joan, who has always wanted to have her own caged birds. Now she's got two of them, a male and a female.

"I can imagine the duets those two will sing!" says her aunt. "Maybe they will even have a family. I wonder?"

Joan is enchanted by them. For hours she watches the two birds jumping and flying in their cage. She is studying them carefully, because she wants to choose suitable names for them.

"But of course! The yellow female shall be called Jonquil, and the orange male shall be Saffron!"

"I hope my mother likes them," says the little girl, anxiously.

28 A Labrador puppy as a present

A shrill, persistent yelping awakens Ann in her little room in her granny's house in the mountains. Ann is spending her Christmas holiday in this lovely, wooden house.

The yelping continues and Ann, now wide awake, realizes happily what it is. It is the adorable, little puppy she got for Christmas! He is a splendid Labrador retriever, with a coat as shiny as silk, all black. He has two big affectionate, trusting eyes. There can be no doubt about it, this puppy has a very nice personality!

29 Matthew receives a tortoise

Among all his other presents on Christmas morning, Matthew also found a tortoise. He already had a goldfish, so now he has another little pet to look after. He immediately gives a name to his new pet: Tammie.

He doesn't know exactly why, but he likes the sound of this name. Matthew likes to look at the precise, geometrical patterns on Tammie's shell, or carapace. And he feels very affectionate every time Tammie timidly sticks out its flat head.

30 Meet Bonbon, the hamster

Clare, like lots of other children, loves animals. Everyone is aware of this and so, for Christmas, she too has a new friend.

It is a hamster, and it is so small you can hardly see it. It has soft fur, brown on the back and reddish further down. Its throat, paws, the insides of its ears, and tip of its nose are a clean white color. It has the sharp teeth of a rodent and front legs ending in real, little hands, with four fingers.

Clare immediately gives a name to her hamster: Bonbon. Along with the little animal, she also received a roomy blue cage. Even though it looks harmless and defenseless, Bonbon would be capable of causing all sorts of trouble and chaos if it was loose around the house. Even though its teeth are very small, it is still capable of nibbling, tearing, chewing, and biting everything that it finds in its path; slippers, books, rugs, curtains, cushions... So Bonbon cannot be left to wander around the house alone.

So beware! For the peace of the family, it is better if Bonbon stays in its lovely, new, blue cage.

31 Searching for a chestnut tree

The cold is biting. Well wrapped in their warm jackets, woollen caps, scarves, and gloves, Peter, Mark, and Clare head off towards the woods. What can they be going to do in this cold? Especially since they are also carrying a basket between them!

The three children walk with their noses in the air, looking up at the tree tops. All of a sudden, they stop at the bottom of a large chestnut tree. Peter gets ready to climb up into it. It becomes more and more strange, this winter outing in the woods...!

1 Greetings under the mistletoe

Many shouts of "Best wishes" and "Happy New Year" ring out in the festive household. At the door to the dining room, beneath a big bunch of mistletoe, everyone, moms and dads, sons and daughters, friends and relatives, all exchange the most affectionate greetings. The New Year begins under a sign of peace and serenity, which is what the mistletoe stands for. This tradition is honored every year.

Yesterday, Peter climbed up onto the lower branches of the big chestnut tree and gathered a few sprigs of mistletoe. There was as much of it as he wanted. To be honest, the chestnut is infested with this parasitic plant, which, even though it is considered a good luck charm, is also harmful to the plant on which it grows, because it draws sustenance away from it.

Peter broke off a fine spray of mistletoe very delicately so that the shiny white berries didn't fall off, and then he passed it down to Clare, who also took care not to touch the berries, because they are poisonous. The children returned home, with bright red noses and some fine pieces of good luck mistletoe.

2 The colorful fruit bowl

All the trees are naked in the garden. In the orchard, the trees have a desolate aspect. The raspberry and redcurrant bushes now look dry and stunted. The strawberry plants don't look too healthy either. Some have yellowing leaves, and others are all damp and limp.

In this grey setting, one gets the impression that life has departed for good, that the trees will never again be covered by leaves, or bear fruit.

As a contrast to the sadness outside, the inside of the house has been brightly decorated with all the colors which bring the summer to mind. Jars of different types of jam have appeared on the table, as well as jars of vegetables preserved in oil, filled with yellow and green peppers and violet-colored aubergines.

Pride of place on the dining room table is given to a big, blue, glass fruit bowl, filled with shiny red apples, pears, and oranges. In the center sits a big pineapple with its pennant of green leaves. There are even some kiwi fruits, with their dull skins, and a big, brown, hairy coconut.

3 A New Year bouquet

Mother has received a lovely bunch of flowers, all arranged very nicely and tastefully. They were delivered wrapped up in a sheet of transparent paper. Inside was a basket covered in colored paper: green on the front and pink on the back; so that along the edge both colors blended together.

As for the flowers, there were delicate mimosas, white and pink carnations, and finally a little apricot-colored rose, very unusual, with a sweet scent. A lovely New Year bouquet from Dad!

4 The world in hemispheres

This is a story about hemispheres. Hemispheres? The word is less complicated than it appears at first sight.

"Hemi" means half. "Sphere" means ball, as in a globe of the world. And so a hemisphere is equal to half a sphere, half of a globe. And since the Earth is a huge globe, each hemisphere is equal to half of the world. The top half is called the northern hemisphere; the bottom half is the southern hemisphere.

Britain, France, the rest of Europe, the United States and Canada, for example, are in the northern hemisphere. Countries like Brazil, Argentina, and Australia, and those in Southern Africa are in the southern hemisphere.

The differences in climate of the two hemispheres are caused by their different seasons: when it is winter in the northern hemisphere, it is summer in the southern hemisphere, and vice-versa.

In reality, the Sun always sends out its rays in a constant manner; but what happens is that the Earth changes its position with respect to the Sun; and, while it rotates around it, the Earth exposes first the northern hemisphere and then the southern one, and so on, to the sun's direct rays.

5 The snow falls steadily

During the morning, the sky had been a uniform, milky-grey color. It was so still that it looked as if it was hiding something, and it stayed that way for hours.

Then, all of a sudden, at lunch time, this overcast sky unfolded its secret and it began to let fall a few small, isolated flakes of snow. But, by evening, they had become thousands, millions of flakes, and they had grown to the size of pieces of torn paper, falling violently and in a steady pattern onto the ground.

6 The lucky piece of bread

A bean, do you know what that is? It is a sort of large seed. There is an ancient tradition in many countries concerning beans. On this day of the Epiphany, people make a special bread. But before it is put in the oven to be cooked, a large bean is placed in the dough. Whoever finds this bean will be lucky in the year to come, and on this day will also receive a prize of a crown or a garland.

That is the ancient tradition. Today a little doll is put in the dough, or a star, or a little new moon shape, or a little heart.

7 The hungry blackbird

The whole garden is covered in snow. The soft cloak of blinding white snow, which spreads over the lawn, the road and the woods nearby, is an enchanting sight to behold.

The snowflakes manage to land so gracefully on every branch, shrub, and stalk, turning them a pure white color.

At dinner time, Clare and Mark look out of the window. The sun is already setting, leaving a pink reflection on the layer of snow.

"Oh look!" exclaims Clare suddenly. Over the white snow, there hops a blackbird, cold and alone.

"It's coming closer to the house," says Mark.

"Perhaps it's hungry," says Clare, feeling sorry for it. "Yes, it must be starving, the poor thing!"

"Let's give it some crumbs," suggests Mark.

The two children slowly open the window and throw some crumbs from the buns they are eating out onto the snow.

The blackbird doesn't wait to be asked twice, and immediately starts pecking away at this unexpected windfall.

8 The blue larks on the window ledge

Every day the blue larks come a little closer to the house. They become more and more brave, and in the end they even make timid jumps onto the window ledge. Sometimes they even tap on the window pane with their little beaks.

Jenny enjoys watching them, though she feels sorry for them out in the cold.

"They must be very hungry!" she exclaims. "I have to do something for these little birds," she decides, her conscience bothering her. And she hurries to get some crumbs for them.

9 The long-tailed crow

Clare has a bad cold. An insistent, hacking cough has been bothering her throughout the whole night, and the night before, and the one before that as well. She cannot go to school, and has to stay in bed, taking horrible medicines and hot drinks.

Pudding, her friendly, playful kitten, is pleased with the situation. He hates going out and getting his paws wet, even if it is just on to the terrace. He does not like all this snow. Better to stay in the warmth of the house, and, between one snooze and another, invent some new games.

Clare, on the contrary, loves to see everything so white outside, and when she is no longer confined to bed, she spends a lot of time looking out of the window. With her nose pressed up against the glass, she contemplates the magical landscape. Then she spies a big crow, with its characteristic black and white plumage. It is rapidly crossing the garden, brushing the powdery snow with its long tail and leaving a regular fan-shaped track with it.

It is a real giveaway, this track, a clear sign that lets everybody know that a crow has been here!

10 A little birdhouse

Clare and her mother discuss how to help all those little birds which come into their garden on these freezing cold days.

"There should be a little wooden house down in the cellar which was made a long time ago for just this purpose," says her mother.

"Oh yes, let's go and look for it," begs Clare.

The little wooden house is found in the cellar, a bit dusty but still whole and solid. It has a sloping roof and a little heart-shaped window to let light in. Clare and her mother go to the store to buy some supplies for the birds: rice, millet, sunflower seeds... and a fair-sized piece of lard. Then the little girl and her mother look for the best place to put up the bird house in the garden. Finally, they find the perfect spot, a fork in the trunk of the chestnut tree. They hang the piece of lard from a shrub branch. Clare puts the seed outside the bird house and spreads some breadcrumbs on the snow.

A short time later, flocks of little birds gather around those unexpected offerings. Clare and her mother get such pleasure from seeing them hopping around wildly, as if competing to see who can eat the most.

11 The squirrel's tracks

Ever since the woods have been covered by a thick layer of snow, the squirrels at the top of the fir tree have been trying to keep warm by wrapping themselves up in their thick tails and cuddling up close to each other. They listen to the silence of the forest, but they don't give in to the long sleep. They don't want to be like the marmots: the squirrels do not want to hibernate.

The poor things are still hungry, and so they have to keep busy to ease the pangs in their tummies. But that is not easy in the winter! So, early each morning, the squirrels come down from their nests to go and look for something to chew on. Since this activity goes on in the dim light of dawn, it is very rare that anyone catches sight of them. That is why it was believed for a long time that squirrels do hibernate in the winter.

And so, this morning, a squirrel, with its flowing red tail, deftly climbs down the frozen tree trunk. When it reaches the snow-covered ground it leaves little star-shaped footprints. Then it silently hops off beneath branches laden with snow. Nobody sees it, nobody hears it!

12 Finding a supply of food

As we know, squirrels are very far-sighted animals and they always build up a supply of food for the cold months. However, they often forget where they have hidden it.

That is what happened to our little squirrel. In the autumn, it had hidden many stores of food, and now it can't even find one of them! But if it wants to stop the rumbling in its stomach, it has to keep on looking. First of all, it searches at random, trusting in good luck. But since its luck is not so good today, it tries hard to remember where it put its supplies. It removes a thick layer of snow and methodically rummages through the roots, through the clods of frozen earth. All of a sudden, the sharp cry of a jay interrupts its fruitless search.

"Oh, don't annoy me!" mumbles the squirrel. "This is not the right moment!" But the cry continues. Growing curious, the little animal decides to take a few steps towards the source of the noise. That is when it notices a big chestnut root sticking out of the snow. Here, in a hollow, it finds two nuts, an acorn and three pieces of mushroom: a whole meal in itself!

"Thank you, thank you, dear jay!" says the little squirrel, running off happily.

13 Birds that remain in the winter

Today I want to introduce you to some of my friends, the little birds who frequent the garden. They haven't abandoned me, in spite of the cold, the snow, and all the hardships of the winter. Instead, they continue to sing bravely, despite the bad weather and the grey skies.

You have already met some of them: the sparrow and the finch, the woodpecker and the robin, the thrush and all the larks and chickadees.

14 Fighting the cold

The temperature has dropped even further. It has stopped snowing and the sky has gradually brightened to a clear blue. During the night, the stars shine like diamonds, but the cold is intense. Huge, transparent icicles hang from the rooftops. Here and there, large patches of ice cover the pavement.

Skip, the dog, withdraws as far as possible to the back of his house, where, to help him cope with the cold, he has been given an old blanket. The temperature is so low, that it even wakes up the hedgehog who has been sleeping for some time now under the woodpile. The bristly little creature tries to move, to stretch its legs a bit and, after sniffing the freezing air, it decides to go out.

It seems crazy to go out into the crunchy, hardened snow on such a cold day. The poor little hedgehog must have gone mad!

But that is not the case. The hedgehog realizes that, if it doesn't want to die of cold, it will have to make a move.

So off it goes.

One, two, one, two! The brave little hedgehog braces itself and walks out... to fight the cold!

15 The bitter taste of bark

With all this cold and snow, even the vegetable garden "salad bar" isn't offering anything! Goodbye, lovely meals of carrots, garnished with sweet smelling parsley! Goodbye, tasty meals of turnips! There is nothing left to eat. But the hare is still hungry. What can it do?

In order not to die of hunger, the hare has had to resign itself to nibbling on the bark of some trees. It doesn't matter if it is a willow or a walnut tree: both are just as bitter!

Bitter, but, even so, they are better than nothing and much appreciated!

16 The skating hare

The reduced winter rations have weakened the hare, which now spends hours in its shelter, a simple hole in the snow, sleeping, and even dreaming a little.

But when the sun shines through weakly from time to time, the hare feels the urge to go for a walk around its territory.

Today is such a day.

The hare comes out of its den and looks at the frozen scene. Then it takes a run, and launches itself onto the frozen pond, sliding around like a born skater!

17 A dangerous bath for the hedgehog

During the freezing winter days, the hedgehog has to move around in order to fight the cold.

On its outings, this friendly little animal moves along the ditches and the edges of roads. It isn't difficult to find its zig-zagging footprints in the snow.

During its walk this evening, a sudden noise makes it grow cautious. So it changes its route and heads down towards the pond, which is completely frozen over nowadays. There it moves out onto the frozen surface.

Unluckily for it, at that point the ice is very thin and, with a dry crack, it opens up beneath him. "Splash!" The unlucky, little animal slips into the freezing cold water. But it is a good swimmer and it soon manages to use its paws to paddle over to the edge of the pond. But it is still not out of danger. Now it has to clamber up onto the bank, and it cannot get a foothold. The grass is wet with snow and very slippery. Lumps of ice it grabs a hold of, keep breaking off and slipping away.

In the end, with a huge heave, the hedgehog manages to take hold of a root and climb up on to the bank. Safe at last!

18 The long, boring winter

Some of the wild ducks didn't leave the pond in the autumn and their lives are now very boring, with nothing happening. They miss the carefree games of last summer, and the visits they received during the autumn, when they watched the migrating birds get ready to travel south.

The young mallard drake is feeling particularly sad. He wishes he could have gone away as well. Next year, when it is fully grown, he will be able to leave, but now the winter seems endless to him.

19 Prisoner of the ice

To fight off its boredom, the young mallard goes swimming along the edge of the reed patch. The pond is almost completely covered in ice. There are only a few free passages which the ducks make regular use of, to keep the access routes open and avoid becoming prisoners of the ice.

One afternoon, tired of looking at the same scenery all the time, the foolish mallard paddles off. He wants to discover new horizons... and so he swims, further and further, without stopping. He has never been this far away. That old willow tree over there, for example; he has never seen it before, nor has he seen that boat moored among the reeds. The young mallard realizes that he doesn't know where he is anymore! He is totally lost in an unknown place!

Night is beginning to fall, a freezing wind is blowing and it is growing colder all the time. The mallard begins to feel very tired. Heedless of the danger, he sticks his head under his wing and goes to sleep. In the middle of the night, he awakens to find himself stuck tight: a rigid band is holding him firm on all sides. The ice has taken him prisoner!

20 Saved from certain death

At the end of the pond there is an old farmhouse, half-hidden behind the reeds. Thick clouds of smoke billow out of the chimney and float off into the pale sky.

The young mallard caught in the ice is worn out. He has tried to break the tough collar of ice which is trapping him, with his beak, but all his efforts have been in vain. In the end, he has to give up the struggle, and the ice tightens its grip even more on him.

A short time later a slight squeaking can be heard in the air, and a man and a boy come out of the farmhouse and walk along the road beside the pond.

"Oh look! A duck!" exclaims the boy. "It's trapped in the ice. Hurry, let's help it!"

The man picks up a big branch and moves towards the boat moored nearby where the ice is thin. He breaks the ice and pulls the boat in. Then he climbs aboard and sets off towards the helpless bird. When he gets close he breaks the ice around the mallard with the branch, then picks up the bird and returns to the shore.

"Let's get it into the warm house. We'll see if we can't bring it back to life," says the man, while he gently strokes the poor, half-frozen bird.

21 The deep sleep of the hedgehog

After its unintentional swim in the frozen water, and a few other nocturnal outings by the cold light of the moon, the hedgehog decides that it is time to return to its dry shelter, beneath the pile of wood.

This time it really will go to sleep. No more dozing! It has had enough of having its sleep broken, of being suddenly jerked awake.

The wise little animal rolls up into a ball, sticks out its quills and, when its body reaches the right temperature, it falls asleep, this time not to waken until the spring.

22 Lots more salmon

High up along the raging torrent, the large salmon is resting after its long, exhausting journey. It spends a long time completely motionless on a bed of white sand, while the clear water flows past it in a stream of tiny, clear bubbles. The sun's rays filter through the cold water, creating extraordinary light effects.

Slowly the great fish gets its strength back. It has even changed its coloring. It is specially dressed to start a family!

Now its back is dark grey, its stomach purple, with delicate, round rosy spots on the sides. Some red stripes run along its head: an impressive outfit for a big occasion!

Its companion has chosen a particularly sandy part of the stream, and there, with her tail, she has dug out a large shallow hole. In this warm hollow, the female salmon lays her eggs. Then the male comes along to fertilize them. Afterwards, with rapid movements of its large tail, it covers the eggs over with a layer of sand for protection.

There will soon be a big increase in the numbers of salmon!

23 The eagle and the ibexes

With its wings spread wide, the golden eagle soars majestically over immense spaces, slowly circling the high mountain peaks. Down below is a peaceful valley, looking like a part of another world.

All of a sudden, out of a crack in the rock face, comes a herd of ibexes. With their hooves together, they leap with amazing ease from one rock to another. They rise up on their hind legs, shake their horns, and blow through their nostrils. The boisterous herd is an amazing sight!

24 The hidden cave

In a wild, solitary place in the mountains, there is a mound of large rocks. Perhaps it hides the entrance to a cave.

A number of frozen stumps, some chopped-down tree trunks, and branches half buried in the snow obstruct the access to it.

All around, beneath the thick layer of snow, there are upturned clumps of earth, piles of leaves, bushes, and an infinite number of dry twigs. Could this cave be inhabited? And if so, by whom?

25 Inside the bear's den

Here is what we would discover if we were able to have a look inside the mysterious cave.

On a bed of leaves and moss, a female bear is sleeping. She has a huge head, a pointed muzzle, round ears, and shiny, brown fur.

Alongside her, in a cradle of dry grasses, two newborn bear cubs are also sleeping peacefully. One is brown, the other reddish. They were born in the cave only two weeks ago, and they are so small they are no longer than mice. In fact, they don't weigh more than eleven ounces: really tiny, little bears, just like teddy bears.

The cubs' eyesight is not yet perfect, but the mother bear looks after them with great care and attention. She keeps them warm and gives them milk. She only goes out for a very short time to drink. She is not eating any food at all. It is the period of winter hibernation, during which she can find no plants, roots, mushrooms, insects, nor fruits, which make up the normal diet of these big mammals.

So, during the cold months, the she-bear is very weak and awaits the thaw impatiently. At times, when she gets really hungry, she goes out of the cave and rolls a snowball down the hill. By doing this, she hopes to uncover at least a few pine cones, spared by the frost, to gather up and chew on.

It is a long, tiring wait for the good weather. The she-bear wants her cubs to discover the infinite riches of the forest. She wants to teach them to delight in the delicacies offered by the woods, and show them how to find them, when the good weather comes.

"I hope the spring comes soon!" says the big bear, yawning.

26 The mallard regains its strength

The young mallard has been taken into the farmhouse. Warmed by a big wood fire, it slowly gets its strength back. It spreads its wings, stretches its webbed feet, and then raises its head.

It is still recovering from its narrow escape, and now it takes a few tentative steps across the smooth, hard, stone floor.

The duck feels clumsy and out of place. It tries to take off and fly, but it bangs into a wall. "Calm down!" says the man who rescued it. "As soon as you get your strength back, you can return to the pond!"

27 The hamster's expanding cheeks

In common with all other hamsters, Clare's has an odd habit. It fills up its cheeks with supplies of food. It has big pouches in its cheeks and it uses them like shopping bags, or like cupboards.

The first time Clare saw the hamster doing this, she thought it had gone mad. She had given it a piece of carrot, so that it could nibble it at leisure. But, instead, Bonbon hurled himself upon the carrot, grabbed it in his paws and shoved it straight into his mouth. And, to get it all in in one piece, he had to push it in with one of his fingers!

His cheek was swollen right up, so much so that it looked like an inflated balloon.

Clare was very surprised, and also worried for Bonbon. She thought he might suffocate, or choke himself to death. Then, to her great surprise, she saw him scurry into a corner of the cage, and there take the whole piece of carrot out of his cheek, obviously quite unconcerned!

"Hamsters are fitted with a very special pair of expanding cheeks," Clare thinks to herself in amusement.

28 A musical contest

Saffron and Jonquil, Joan's two canaries, spend the winter in the city. The little cage in which they live is placed on a table in front of the glass doors which lead onto the balcony.

Every day, some playful sparrows come and land on the iron railing of the balcony. From that perch, they let out challenging twitterings at the top of their voices. On the other side of the windows, the canaries do not want to be outdone and they reply with their own chirping, twittering songs.

A real musical contest!

29 A day in the life of a tortoise

Tammie the tortoise is spending the winter in an apartment in the city, and he has settled into his new home without any problems.

This is how he spends his day. Since the sound of the vacuum cleaner scares him, in the mornings he takes shelter under the radiator. Later on, when things calm down, he goes for a walk on the shiny floor. Then he goes into the kitchen and lunches on a lettuce leaf. When the sun puts a nice warm patch of light on the floor, he goes and lies in it. In the evening, he loves hiding under the living room rug.

30 Gummy is a lot of work!

Mark wouldn't have believed that the guinea pig he got for Christmas would keep him so busy.

Gummy, that is his name, needs a lot of looking after. First of all, there is his food. His meals are made up of fairly simple foods, but he has to be given the right amount, the right amount, that is, to satisfy a very greedy animal! Gummy eats mixed salads with a variety of carefully selected herbs, together with carrots and crunchy turnips, bits of toasted bread, well-cooked potatoes, slices of apple, and cornflakes. Of course, he also always needs to have a bowl of fresh water available.

A menu like this requires quite a lot of work: but that's not all. Gummy has other needs as well. His little house needs to be cleaned and his straw bed has to be changed every day. Then Mark has to be careful that the delicate little animal is not placed in a drafty area, because he catches cold easily. He also has to be careful that Clare's cat doesn't come too close: it might mistake Gummy for a large mouse and chase him.

What a lot of work for one little guinea pig!

31 Blackie on watch

Blackie, the Labrador puppy, is waiting at the window for his owner. In spite of his short legs – he is still a puppy – he manages go get up onto the sofa, which he is not really allowed to do. He pushes the folds of the curtains aside with his nose and looks outside. The garden, the pavement, the woods, and the hills beyond are all buried under the snow.

All of a sudden, he sees a figure wearing a hat at the end of the path. Blackie leaps around, yelping and wagging his tail. This is how he welcomes Ann home.

1 The salmon sets off again

The salmon's job as father is finished! The preparations to welcome the new family of young fish are also completed. By now, the male salmon is beginning to feel the strain! He is so exhausted that he can only just manage to keep swimming. If it were possible, he would lie down on the sand by the shore and not move another fin!

In spite of this, his love of travel gives him back some energy. He drags himself into the middle of the stream, and gives himself over to the current, which starts to carry him down river.

In this way, without tiring himself out or making any effort at all, he lets himself be carried over the rapids and the whirlpools down the course of the river until he eventually reaches the ocean.

During this lazy voyage, the salmon changes its appearance once again, going back to the silvery color it had in its youth. Once again it looks very much like the young fish that first made its descent towards the sea. Now the salmon is ready to repeat the adventure.

2 The bear's winter rest

The mother bear and the two little cubs spend the winter in a well-sheltered cave.

But where is the father bear in the meantime? Where could he be? Why doesn't he live with his family?

The fact is that the male bear prefers to live alone. He is a complete loner. With the approach of winter, the bear had gone looking for a cave where he could rest during the bad weather. And as soon as he found a suitable one, he began the hard task of preparing it, carrying in branches, grass and moss to make it warm and comfortable. At first the bear doesn't move into it on a permanent basis. He leaves the cave now and then to wander about. But, after the first snowfall, he closes himself inside for good, which also ensures that there is no chance that his tracks will be seen in the snow. The bear stays there sleeping for as long as the winter lasts. However, legend has it that on the second of February each year the bear wakes up to see what the weather is like!

"Ah, it's still winter!" he says. "Oh well, I had better go back to sleep."

3 The well-concealed hare

Across the powdery snow, a clear set of tracks leads to some rough woodland, filled with rocky inclines, bushes, and twisted roots. Let's follow the tracks.

Without making any noise, we approach the place where the tracks disappear. They must lead somewhere! Look! There is a snow-white hare resting on the white snow. Our patience has been rewarded. If you do not actually stumble across it, it certainly isn't easy to spot a hare in the snow-covered winter landscape.

4 The elk's hard winter

The elk from the forests of the north is truly a giant. It has a large head, wide, branching antlers, strong hooves, and a thick bristling coat.

It, too, is impatiently waiting for the winter to end, for a whole lot of reasons. First of all, it wants to get back to swimming in peace. Although it is so huge, the elk loves swimming, and it is quite capable of crossing wide stretches of lakes or the sea.

During the winter, all the water is imprisoned under the ice, and if anything really hates the ice, then it is the elk! If an elk is unlucky enough to slip and fall on a patch of ice, it is incapable of getting up again. So, during this period of the year, the elk abandons the dangerous expanses of ice and takes refuge in the mountains. There it awaits the spring, when it will be able to find its favorite foods again: leaves, young shoots, and slivers of birch bark, and, most of all, moor grasses. Meanwhile, to keep its hunger at bay, the big animal has to eat pine needles. During the winter, the elk also loses its antlers, though they grow back, robust and majestic again, in the spring.

5 The reindeer's winter fur coat

The reindeer has very unusual antlers. They are straight and round at the roots, then they become flat and arch towards the front.

Even the female reindeer wear this massive head-dress. During the winter, this trophy falls off, and doesn't grow back again until the spring. During the cold season, the reindeer's fleece grows thicker with long, shaggy fur, mostly of a light grey color. Thanks to this extra protection, the reindeer can even survive in polar temperatures.

6 Digging for a winter meal

To help it cope with the glacial cold, the reindeer has grown an exceptionally warm coat. But what does it eat? At this time of year, with the snow piled up all over the place, it certainly won't be able to find those tasty, little mushrooms it loves so much, nor the juicy, ripe berries which are so abundant during the warm weather.

For the winter, the reindeer has to make do with a mixture of mosses and lichens, dug out forcibly with its strong hooves from beneath the frozen crust.

7 A snow blanket for the elk

How do you protect yourself from the cold when the temperature drops to less than fifty degrees below zero?

This is a problem which the elk has to solve. Of course, in the winter, it has a special aid to survival in the form of a thicker fur coat. But this does not have the same insulating quality that the reindeer's winter coat has.

And so, the elk has to resort to tricks. It makes itself a cover, a cover of snow! I am not joking! The elk lowers its mighty bulk down beside a bush, tucks its legs in under it, and, bit by bit, allows itself to become covered by the snow. Under the shelter of this pure white cover, it manages to maintain its body heat, and at last can enjoy some rest without freezing up. It really needs rest, because it is worn out by the hardships of the climate, and weakened by the lack of food, due to its enforced fasting.

When it gets its strength back a bit, the elk gets up again, it shakes off the snow and goes for a quick look around. To do this, it follows its own trails through the snow, going round and round in circles!

8 The hare's main roads

As soon as the sun comes out, the hare leaves its burrow and sets off across the blinding, white snow.

Following its natural, deep-rooted instincts, a hare always takes the same trails across the fields and frozen clearings.

In this way, by going backwards and forwards along the same paths, the hare ends up making deep and easily recognizable trails through the snow. These are the hare's main roads.

9 The fox's disturbing cries

At this time of the year, the fox starts to think about finding a mate. It is also the time when the fox can be heard most often.

Perhaps this is so it will be heard for miles, or possibly to attract a mate?

We don't know the correct answer, but we do know, for sure, that during the nights of the month of February, in the country, the strange, unsettling yelping of the fox can be heard. It takes the form of a rough, prolonged bark, followed by a sharp, piercing yelp.

At times, the cries sound like strangled cries and yowling groans, and sometimes as if they are made by an owl. These weird sounds ring out through the frozen, winter nights.

The farm dogs grow alarmed and reply by barking furiously. When the fox approaches an inhabited farm-house, the dogs increase their barking.

When it hears this, the fox begins to grow angry and lets out the most piercing of cries.

Nights like these can be very disturbing!

10 The beavers pass a comfortable winter

Thanks to their foresight, the beavers have a very comfortable winter: they suffer no lack of either food or warmth.

Because of the insulated roof, the temperature inside the lodge remains fairly high; and the snow which also covers it, acts as an extra protection. In the beavers' house, it is warmer during the winter than during the summer. And that is a very happy situation.

As for food, the beavers only have to help themselves from their floating stores, from which they can take a willow branch, a poplar twig, or anything else they choose. If the winter lasts longer than expected, then they can fall back on the supplies that they stored around the entrance to the lodge, below the water level.

When the river is held in the grip of the ice, the beaver stays home resting in its lodge, or it may go out for a swim under the icy crust. From time to time, it will make its way up to the surface to breathe the fresh air through holes that it cuts in the ice. Winter can be quite comfortable for a beaver!

11 The mountaineering chamois

Everyone knows that chamois are exceptionally bold climbers. They are completely at ease climbing up sheer rock faces. With a single bound, they can cross raging streams or waterfalls frozen to dripping icicles.

Another way in which they show themselves to be fine mountaineers is in the care they take not to do anything carelessly. If, for example, they have to make a dangerous jump, they do it one at a time, in this way making sure that any rocks that might be knocked loose do not fall on the chamois that follows.

12 The chamois in search of food

The winter is very harsh. Up on the high mountain peaks, the herd of chamois are having trouble finding enough to eat. Even though she is very wise and experienced, the leading female chamois no longer knows in which direction to lead the herd in order to find lichens hidden under the snow.

It is a large herd, consisting of females, calves, and the youngsters less than three years old. As for the adult males, they prefer to remain separate, either alone or in groups, according to their own individual tastes.

What really lowers the resistance of the chamois is not so much cold, as hunger. The head of the herd is forced to make a decision. They will go down the mountainside. Bravely, she leads the herd down through the fir woods, almost as far as the inhabited areas. Here, a young boy is the first to spot the short, curved horns of the chamois.

"They are hungry, we have to help them," say the people who live on the mountains. "We have to take some bales of hay up to the woods and leave them out for the chamois to eat."

13 The chamois weather forecasters

Two days before a snow storm strikes, the chamois of another valley have left the peaks, and come down to take shelter among the trees in the woods below.

How do they know, two days before?

Because the chamois can "feel" the onset of bad weather, and know just what to do to survive a storm. Before it arrives, they gather together in the forest. Afterwards, when the good weather returns, they move back, up to the mountain tops.

A herd of chamois are as good as a barometer!

14 The deer lose their antlers

The mighty deer, with its huge branching antlers, spends the winter in the forest. Food does not worry it, because the forest is capable of providing it with everything that it needs to live: bark from trees, mistletoe berries, heather, thorn bushes, and even some moss, which can be found growing near streams.

Of course, its winter diet is not as tasty as the one it is used to during the summer. But the deer patiently waits for the spring, when it will be able to enjoy fresh buds, tender grass, and crisp vegetables.

The winter also brings another important change to the stags. They lose their antlers. This usually happens in February. One day its antlers drop off; but it is nothing to worry about, because in May they begin to grow back, with an extra branch. So by the next autumn, the stags' antlers are more beautiful and imposing than they were the year before.

You can actually tell the age of a stag from its antlers. You have to count the points on them. They are called "tines" and there is one for each year of the stag's life.

15 The red deer family

The hinds, the pretty, mild-mannered female deer, and their calves spend their winter in a different way. They keep together in groups in the thickets of trees, sheltered from the wind and the thick snowfalls. The hinds, who, unlike the stags, have no antlers, are wearing their winter coats. The hides, which used to be reddish, smooth, and shiny as silk, have become more grey and more thickly covered.

As for the youngsters, since August they have also lost the distinguishing white spots that dotted their hides.

Stags, hinds, calves... these are all members of the family of red deer. Red deer live throughout Europe, and can also be found in north-west Africa and south-west Asia. When a calf is born in the spring, it is no bigger than a kid, but at the age of six months the sexes begin to differ visibly. Hinds grow larger but otherwise show little change, while the young stags develop two humps on their forehead during their first winter. These humps become their antlers, which continue to grow year after year.

16 The swallows' golden winter

When the roofs, balconies, and terraces of our houses are covered by a thick coat of snow, there is no sign of our friendly swallows.

They are spending the winter in Africa, among tropical plants, luxuriously growing beneath the warm rays of the equatorial sun. Some swallows even fly down as far as the southern tip of the African continent. While we are wrapped up in warm jackets, they are spreading their wings in the hot sun and tasting all the different varieties of insects which fly around in such great numbers.

17 The storks' two routes to the sun

Some storks are moving along the shores of a sun-drenched lake. These large birds, with their long, bright red legs and long, red, pointed beaks, are a magnificent sight. They have enormous, white wings tipped with black feathers. Although they have hardly any voice, they can still make themselves clearly heard by clacking the two halves of their beaks together... Storks are also birds which enjoy a reputation for being bearers of good luck.

Storks nest not only in central, northern and eastern Europe, but also in the south of Spain. They build their nests on the roofs of houses, and in those places where it is usual for them to make their nests, you will hear people saying: "The storks are coming," or "The storks are leaving."

But where are they coming from? And where are they going?

As early as the month of August, when it is beginning to get cooler in the north of Europe, the storks start their journey back to southern Africa. There, the climate is warm, and on the banks of the big, swampy lakes the storks can find the food they prefer: frogs, water snakes, little fish, and aquatic insects. To return to these wintering places they always follow the same routes. If we look at a map, we can see these routes quite easily. One is the western route which crosses France, Spain, and the Straits of Gibraltar, into Africa. The other is the eastern route, which goes through the whole of eastern Europe and then over the Bosphorous, and down to the Suez Canal.

We know about these two routes because experts in northern Europe put small, identifying rings on the young storks' legs. At various points along the way, the storks are captured briefly and their rings checked. In the end, they will have traveled many thousands of miles from their nests.

18 The storks leave Africa

In February, the storks leave the big, sun-baked lake and set off to return to the north again. They are going back to the same nests that they left the previous year. They are a magnificent sight as they take off. Their lovely, white wings turn out to be very large when they are open wide, a spread of more than six feet.

In order to take off and lift their body mass from the ground, storks have to take a run up, consisting of short jumps – hop! hop! hop! – faster and faster, until finally they manage to get up into the air.

19 The storks as gliders

You would imagine that it would be exhausting to have to fly for so many miles! Fortunately for the storks, it is not as bad as it seems. They have learned how to make use of the rising currents of hot air to help them fly.

After their first run up, and take off from the ground, the rising hot air helps to take them up high. Since they are expert fliers, the storks spread their wings wide and let the "cushion" of hot air keep them aloft. In order to keep going in the right direction, they only have to tilt one or other of their wings from time to time.

In this way, the storks fly high up in the sky, almost as if they were gliders, calm, silent, and almost still. They pass over lakes, swamps, meandering rivers, and the wide, golden plain.

It must be a fantastic journey. And, as the evening falls, the air cools down so the warm currents can no longer keep them aloft. The storks slowly glide down to earth, where they will spend the night, underneath the palm trees which line the banks of the winding rivers, beside the sweet tinkling of the waters.

20 The storks' resting places

Sometimes, storks will even stop in the same place for several days, in order to rest. If they stop on the banks of a river, they keep very still for a long time, waiting for an unlucky little fish to swim along. Or else, they might wander through the palm trees, pecking away at a lizard here, a mouse there, or even tasty, brightly colored insects. During these restful pauses, the storks take full advantage of all the good things they can find to eat!

21 The unusual trio

More curious than their companions, two storks have left the group and wandered off into the cultivated fields. Balancing on their long, thin legs, they follow the furrows in the ground, stopping often to grab a crunchy grasshopper or a tasty snail, with a quick peck of their beaks. Suddenly, behind a tall eucalyptus tree with wide, perfumed leaves, they see a donkey and a camel, with its big hump. At the sight, the two storks stop to have a look.

The little donkey and the large camel, with its thick, sand-colored fur, are pulling a simple wooden plow, held by an African peasant. The farmer is wearing a typical African, striped tunic with a hood, made out of a material, called barracan in Arabic, of wool and goat's hair.

Without hesitation, the two storks begin to follow this strange threesome, at the same time taking advantage of the newly-plowed furrow to grab the insects that are revealed as the earth is turned.

22 Why not stay in Africa?

When they pause to rest in the north African city of Marrakesh, some of the storks in the group, which is heading for Alsace, in France, decide to end their journey there, and remain where they are.

They are afraid that far away in Europe they will not be able to find the abundance and variety of food that exists in this warm country: grasshoppers and crickets, tadpoles and frogs, fish, snakes, and lizards, all in abundance. Furthermore, there is more light and warmth in Marrakesh, and there is already a large colony of storks nesting here happily. They lay their eggs, brood over them, and raise their young beneath the warm rays of the African sun. The temptation to follow their example is very strong. After all, perhaps when they get to Alsace, they might find themselves to be the only pair of storks in the village. That would be sad and lonely!

All these considerations lead one little group to decide to remain in Marrakesh. They begin at once to build their nests, which they have decided to locate high up on the fortifications of the old city. From there, they can look down on everything, and launch themselves easily into the air.

23 The cattle egret and the sacred ibis

Not only the storks enjoy a happy stay in Africa. Lots of other birds, who also travel, have discovered the sun-filled lands there and visit them regularly. Such birds are the herons, the spoonbills with their flat beaks, and the glossy ibis, with its purple-bronze sheen.

When they visit Africa, these birds find themselves in the company of others of their species which live there permanently; like the cattle egrets, which like to graze amidst the hooves of cattle, and the sacred ibis, which was a god to the ancient Egyptians.

24 The flamingo, the "firebird"

There is a Russian fairy tale about a firebird. It is believed that the bird which is the Greater Flamingo, which lives today not only in Africa but also in some European countries. The Greater Flamingo is best known for its multi-shaded pink coloring. In olden days, the bird was also called "wings of fire".

It has long, thin legs, of a bright pink color, delicate, pale, pink plumage, and huge wings with fiery red-colored reflections. It also has a long flexible neck, gracefully arched downwards, and a beak which is both ornamental and of great practical use: ornamental because it is colored red and black; practical in as much as it is equipped with a kind of internal strainer that allows it to filter the water, while keeping in the fish, especially tiny ones.

When in flight, the Greater Flamingo stretches out its neck and sticks out its legs, beating its wings rapidly. These gorgeous birds travel in large flocks, and as they fly, the sky becomes tinged with pink. A truly wonderful, unforgettable sight!

25 A beautiful contrast

The favorite dwelling-place of the flamingos is among the reeds, on the banks of shallow ponds, between plants and aquatic grasses. In these surroundings, flamingos move gracefully, bending their heads with every step and sticking their beaks under the water to catch the tiny crabs and shellfish on the bottom that they live on.

The green-blue color of the water sets off the extraordinary plumage of the Greater Flamingos, bringing out in contrast all their various shades of pink.

26 The mallard is set free

Do you wonder what happened to the young mallard that was found by its two rescuers nearly frozen to death on the lake?

It was kept in the warmth of the house and well-fed for a few days, and then it was released in a sheltered part of the pond. It was very happy to be free again!

The fortunate duck began happily swimming, with all the water fowl, like the long-tailed ducks, that come down from the north to spend the winter in a less harsh climate.

27 The truly inseparable kingfishers

The river where the pair of kingfishers made a home is now covered by a thick layer of shiny ice, imprisoning its waters, while the banks appear to be asleep under the white blanket of snow.

Everything has been hardened and made rigid by the cold: not a bough is bending nor a branch swaying, nor a blade of grass moving. In the midst of all this cold stillness, the only sign of life is the rapid, darting flight of the two kingfishers, male and female, who have remained in an enchanted landscape to face the hardships of winter.

It is possible to see the pair of them darting over the surface of the ice, or sitting on a tree branch. They can sometimes be seen sitting on the snow-capped top of a rock, or busily climbing up the river bank.

The two kingfishers never leave each other: it seems that they are unable to live without each other.

Now that the river is frozen, they land on the ice-hard surface, and with repeated pecks of their beaks, they try to make a hole, so that they can catch their daily supply of fish. Underneath this solid sheet of ice-armor, the river continues to flow as always.

After they have eaten, the inseparable couple continue their trip. This is the way that kingfishers spend their winter, awaiting the return of spring.

The two birds are so attached to each other that if one of them becomes ill the other dedicates all its efforts to making it well again. If its efforts are all in vain and its companion dies, the survivor hurries off and hides itself in a corner. There, without flying or eating any more, the remaining bird gives out pathetic, little, sorrowing chirps, until it too dies. Kingfisher couples really are inseparable!

28 The parrot opposite

Today I looked out of the window. In the opposite apartment, I saw a large parrot, perched on a bamboo swing inside a large roomy cage. There was this exotic parrot in an apartment in the city in the middle of winter! When the world is still so grey, a brightly-colored parrot makes you think of the good weather to come.

That parrot seemed to be the most beautiful bird I could imagine. Its feathers were a delicate, pearl-grey color, and it had a flashy, black and red tail. Its strong, hooked beak was a shiny black color. I looked that parrot up in my bird book. It turned out to be an African Grey Parrot which lives in the equatorial forests of Africa. It must be very unhappy in our climate, the poor bird, I thought.

The sight of this parrot led me to spend a long time staring across at the window of the opposite apartment. This was certainly good for my knowledge of African Grey Parrots, but it wasn't very good for my homework!

29 The musical chestnut tree

In the woods outside the garden of Clare's house, there is a huge chestnut tree. It is a tree like lots of others, with a solid trunk, marked with long furrows, and with strong, thick, main branches, and a healthy growth of secondary branches.

But this tree is better loved than any of the others, because it is a musical chestnut tree. It plays host in its branches to a whole variety of singing birds. If you listen carefully, you can hear them chirping, twittering and cheeping, day and night, all through the year.

Each different bird sings in its own tone and timbre, and they have settled into the tree at different levels. Here the blue lark is singing in its trilling voice. There, well-hidden, is a jay, with its penetrating cry. Higher up, a pair of collared doves are cooing. At the top, another jay deafeningly replies. In the angle of a large branch, a red wood-pecker is playing the drums. From out of a hole in the trunk, a long-eared owl speaks with a deep, somber voice into the dark night, its moaning hoot echoing through the woodlands.

Yes, the big chestnut tree is a place where you can be sure of hearing a variety of music, even if not all of it is to your taste!

1 The elk versus the mosquito!

You'll never guess what an elk is scared of! What do you think it is that frightens this giant animal with its mighty horns? It wanders out at will, through the birch forests of the north, and the mysterious swamps, yet it is scared of... what?

It is terrified of mosquitoes! The mighty elk is scared of the bites of these little insects – because they can drive it crazy with desperation and pain, the tiny, but powerful, mosquito!

2 The hedgehog's most deadly enemy

"And now, try and guess, if you can, what is the worst enemy of the hedgehog?"

"Is it the weasel's relative, the polecat, with its sharp teeth?"

"No, it's not the polecat."

"Well, maybe the owl, that predator of the night?"

"No, its not the owl."

"Perhaps it is the fox, that scavenger that prowls all night long through the woods and fields?"

"No, it's not the fox."

"Well then, is it the wild boar, with its fearsome tusks?"

"No, not him either."

The hedgehog's biggest enemies are cars! The harmless little hedgehog, with all its quills, loves to linger on paved roads that have been warmed by the sun. When a car comes along, instead of running away, the hedgehog curls itself up into a ball, just as it always does when faced with danger. However, this instinctive move does not protect the hedgehog in this case.

3 A fox goes frog hunting

The fox has a very simple, yet clever, way of fishing for frogs. The cunning animal sits down on the river bank as if it was there for a rest. Then it lets its thick tail dangle in the water of the pond or the stream. The careless frogs are attracted to the ruddy reflections of the tail, and swim over and take hold of it. The fox quickly pulls its tail out of the water, and snaps up the hapless frogs, one by one!

176

4 How far can a ladybug fly?

"Do you have any idea how far a tiny ladybug can fly?"

"About the distance between one bright flower and another along the edge of the garden?"

"No, much more than that!"

"Well then, the distance from the flower bed to the hedge of lilac?"

"No, much more!"

"Well, in that case, I'd guess that it would be possible for a ladybug to fly across the road to another garden."

"No, ladybugs can go further than that!"

"Well, maybe from the gardens at one end of the road to the gardens at the other end."

"No, much more!"

"Surely a ladybug wouldn't be able to fly all the way across the park to the gardens on the other side?"

"Oh yes, much more than that!"

"I give up then. I don't know how far a ladybird can fly."

"Well, it seems difficult to believe, but it is really true. A little ladybug is capable of flying across the English Channel, from England to France. That is about thirty miles in a straight line. Of course, it doesn't do this alone, but with others in a cloud. It's an amazing achievement."

5 The panic-stricken flamingos

Flamingos are among the most picturesque and beautiful of all the birds in the world. They have longer legs and necks in proportion to their bodies than any other birds. Their feeding methods are unique. The birds feed with their top bill at the bottom and the lower bill above pumping against it to sieve their food out of the water through slits in the top bill.

If you then consider the beautiful plumage of the flamingos, you will appreciate, even more, how important it is that these birds should survive, and that their numbers should increase.

One of the main dangers to their survival is the sound of engines, especially aircraft engines. Flamingos are so terrified by this noise that they panic at once. If it happens near a breeding colony, the birds go into a frenzy and fly away immediately, leaving behind their eggs and their young!

6 Two mice talking

"Where will you spend the winter, my friend?" a long-tailed mouse asked a mouse with a very short tail.

"I'm staying in my burrow!" replied the little mouse with the short tail. "The apartment where I live is just perfect for me. The badger who lives on the floor below doesn't bother me at all. Of course, he spends most of his time asleep, and only goes out once in a while for a drink. As for me, I have a large supply of acorns, so there's nothing to make me go outside!"

"I am going to do what I did last year," replied the long-tailed mouse. "I'll go back into the farmer's house. It is nice and warm there... and the cupboards are always full. I spend hours in them. It's true that the dog is grumpy, but deep down he isn't a bad old fellow. He certainly can't be bothered chasing after me. And, best of all, there aren't any cats!"

After their chat, the two mice each set off in their different directions to go to their winter homes.

And how are they doing now? Did they stick to their plans? You can be sure that they did. Mice are animals who keep their word!

7 Comfortably settled in the barn

For some reason, I have found myself wondering a lot recently about that family of fieldmice that we met last summer. What has happened to those tiny, feather-light creatures? Where are they spending their winter?

What could have become of them after their wheat-field was harvested? Where could they have taken refuge?

The spider, who has his big web in the barn, told me the news about them, so that I don't have to worry any more.

"Don't you fret about them," said the spider, interrupting his weaving for a moment. "The little fieldmice have been living here since the end of the autumn. They turned up one rainy night, soaking wet, and scuttled in here as fast as their little legs could carry them. They immediately set up a comfortable home for themselves behind the garden tools. I don't know how they did it, but they found bits of paper and rags to make up nice, soft beds. As for food, all they have to do is take their pick from the huge stores of wheat!"

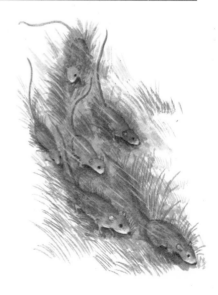

8 Guests in the henhouse

The red hen was telling me: "If you are looking for the fieldmice, you should know that quite a few families have made homes with us in the henhouse. Ever since the weather turned cold, they have been quietly creeping in through the fence. They have even been helping themselves to our food, drinking out of our dishes, racing all over the place. They even go out into the farmyard. Sometimes they can be bullies. We just show them our beaks and warn them to behave, because, after all, it is our henhouse!"

9 The wise country mouse

The hardy, little country mouse has no problems overcoming the hardships of the cold season.

Long before the start of the winter, it had filled up its store cupboard with supplies. The country mouse lives in a burrow which it digs in the field. The burrow has several entrances, lots of tunnels, and a large number of rooms. Some of the tunnels lead to rooms used for storing supplies.

The far-sighted country mouse began to fill them up in the autumn with plant roots, onion bulbs, potatoes, and lots of other things it likes to eat. All these supplies were stored with those it had already put aside during the summer: plants, grain, and various types of seeds. Everything was gathered together in the storerooms, along with the wheat taken after the harvest.

The wise little country mouse also took leaves into its den to line it against the cold. During the month of January, he and his mate decided to increase their family. In the coming spring, there will be an extra happy occasion for them with the birth of lots of other country mice. It will be a very happy springtime for the mice!

10 Work, work, and still more work

You mustn't think that the frost has stopped the mole from working. Nothing stops this tireless, little digger of tunnels.

In a place where the snow has melted, Matthew found a whole series of freshly-made piles of earth this morning. Not only does the mole continue to dig, but, at the beginning of March, it also completes building its nest, a round chamber furnished with dry leaves, with two tunnel entrances. This is where the next family of earth-digging moles will be born.

11 The garden comes back to life

The snow has been gone from Clare's garden for several weeks now, and it looks sad and barren. After its long winter rest, the grass is all crushed and flattened, looking like dry hay. This will not be the case for long. The covering of snow only damaged it on the surface: now it will start to grow healthy and strong again.

In fact, a few bright green shoots are already showing up here and there, and the first spring daisies are beginning to sprout.

12 The ants' mating flight

The winter freeze which made the earth as hard as stone is finished now. After their enforced rest, the fields come back to life and the warmth of the sun makes the grass start to grow again.

The insects also begin to reappear, by the thousands. They are already extremely busy, racing up and down the new blades of grass, waving their little antennae wildly, as they hurry off to keep their mysterious appointments.

One of the species of insect to appear is the black ant. They seem to move around even more than the others, hurrying along on their way, paying no attention at all to the fresh, green, dew-covered buds. There must be a reason why they are in such a rush. We had better not distract them or get in their way!

A stalk of hay lying across the path irritates the ants terribly. They wave their antennae, then they climb over it and continue on their way. Where can they be going? Ants have a lot of secrets. We ought to try and find out something about them.

Do you know that there are "queen ants", that are very big and have wings? On a certain day, these queen ants celebrate their own kind of "wedding", to male ants that also have wings. They take to the sky by the thousands on their "honeymoon" trip! But the marriages last less than a day!

After this flight, the queens lose their wings and go under ground to lay eggs and set up an ant colony. The males die after the flight! It is the end of their life cycle.

Queen ants, on the other hand, can live for about twenty years. They lay thousands of eggs, out of which hatch the first ants of a new colony each year.

13 A life of constant work

After she has laid her eggs, the queen ant personally takes care of the cocoons and the larvae, helping to bring the new ants into the world. But, as time goes by, and the number of worker ants increases, the hard-working queen begins to grow tired. She allows herself to be fed, served and completely cared for by the workers.

Worker ants work all their lives without respite. They serve as nurses, harvesters, carpenters, and guards, doing everything in a well-organized, disciplined way.

14 The salmon's adventures

Do you remember the adventurous salmon? It was born in the river, then swam down to the sea. Then the salmon swam across the ocean, exploring it along the way. Afterwards, it swam back up to its home river, fertilized the eggs laid by the female, and then let itself be carried by the current, down the river and back to the sea.

In the water of the estuary, the silvery fish once again experiences the salty taste of the sea. The flavor of shrimps and crabs in the water not only gives it back its appetite, but also its strength! Once again, the salmon is impatient to be on its way across the vast ocean. Once again, the salmon will travel the great underwater routes, where no human can follow it, swim in the powerful ocean currents, and leap in the whirlpools, the surf, the waves, and the tides. It will wander through thick forests of algae, and there, in the murky depths of the ocean, it may remain for the rest of its life.

Or, it might go back, once again, to the river where it was born. It might, once more, swim back up that river against the current. There are some salmon who make this incredible return journey up to three times in the course of their adventurous lives.

15 Nature reawakens

As soon as the first tender buds begin to show on the dry branches of the bushes, we are aware that all of nature is beginning to wake up.

The skylark is the first to celebrate the return of life. It lifts off into the blue sky, and flies above before once again returning to land on a branch that seems lifeless.

Even the snail, that has spent the whole winter down at the bottom of its shell, pokes its head out once again, and slowly makes its way back to the river's edge.

16 A blackbird in the city

Normally, I am awakened in the mornings by the subdued, insistent chirping of blackbirds in the chestnut tree outside my bedroom window. But I am staying in the city now, and I was awakened by a city blackbird singing a song. This didn't surprise me, because it is the middle of March, and, by this time, city blackbirds are singing their spring songs. Country blackbirds begin theirs later.

17 Uncertain March weather

The birds in the gardens and parks do not know where to take shelter: the weather is playing a lot of nasty tricks on them.

To start with, a heavy shower of rain fell on them without any warning. There was no chance to prepare for it! No sooner had the birds hurried off to take shelter in a tree, the sky cleared, and a warm, bright sun came out. The weather was making fun of them! But the birds didn't lose their patience. Instead they shook the water off their soaking feathers and flew back out into the sunshine.

This sudden, unexpected warmth is very welcome! The birds sing out their joy... but in no time at all the sky turns a threatening, dark color again. There is another surprise on its way. Suddenly huge hailstones, as big as pigeon eggs, come hammering down from out of the black clouds.

Hiding under the eaves, an old crow croaks philosophically: "Just March showers, I suppose!"

18 The signs of spring

If the blackbird is early in announcing the arrival of spring, then the horse-chestnut tree in the garden is not far behind. At the first hint of spring, it covers itself with lovely, little, pink and green buds.

All the other horse-chestnuts on the street are still bare and are just beginning to sprout small, resinous buds, still totally closed.

For all these big trees, though, it is only a matter of days. Suddenly, one day, beautiful fans of palm-shaped leaves will open.

19 The storks fly overhead

When it is once again the time for the storks to fly, cries of joy and shouts of happiness can be heard all around.

These big birds always receive an enthusiastic welcome. Children point at them and wave, as if it were some kind of miracle, shouting: "The storks are passing over; good luck is on its way!" Even the grown-ups raise their heads from their work, look up at them and feel a sudden happiness. The elderly are especially moved, and their thoughts drift back to days-gone-by, to all the years they have watched the storks fly over in the past.

Meanwhile, the storks continue on their way, without stopping, determinedly flying on. They have to get back to the nests they abandoned last year.

When the currents of hot air are forced to give way to cooler ones, or when a contrary wind blows, the storks are forced to beat their big, white wings with their black fringes harder to keep going in the right direction. They struggle on, but their powers of endurance are strained. The journey back from the wintering lands in Africa has been a long one. But the storks are determined to get back to find their nests.

20 The return of the storks

The storks have continued on their way throughout the whole day. They have left huge forests behind, they have followed the courses of sparkling rivers and flown over peaceful villages.

Some of them have stopped off along the way. Those birds have already reached their destinations. Unlike on their migration to the south, when they return, storks do not fly in large flocks, but in small groups. The group that we are following gradually becomes smaller and smaller, until, one evening, there are only two left.

With the last, tired beats of the wings, these two storks finally reach their destination. At the end of a wide valley, they see "their" village.

They begin to glide down, with their wings spread wide and their long, red beaks pointing downwards.

The soft, gentle storks recognize their old nest right away, beside the chimney stack on a high, sloping-roofed house.

Worn out from their journey, they descend and click their beaks together in happiness. All the children in the valley run towards the lucky house to joyfully welcome back the beautiful, feathered bearers of good luck.

The winter is the surprise hidden in a basket of nuts and dried fruits: walnuts, hazelnuts and almonds, raisins, sultanas, and apricots, and other sweet fruits dried in the sun.

The winter is a lovely basket of fresh fruits from all over the world: juicy pineapples with the joyous plumes of leaves, grapefruit and pomegranates, bananas, kiwi fruit, and oranges, which bring the color of the sun to the table.

The winter means silence in the mountains and a warm den to take shelter in. The white blanket of snow protects the animals and the seeds, and prevents them from becoming frozen.

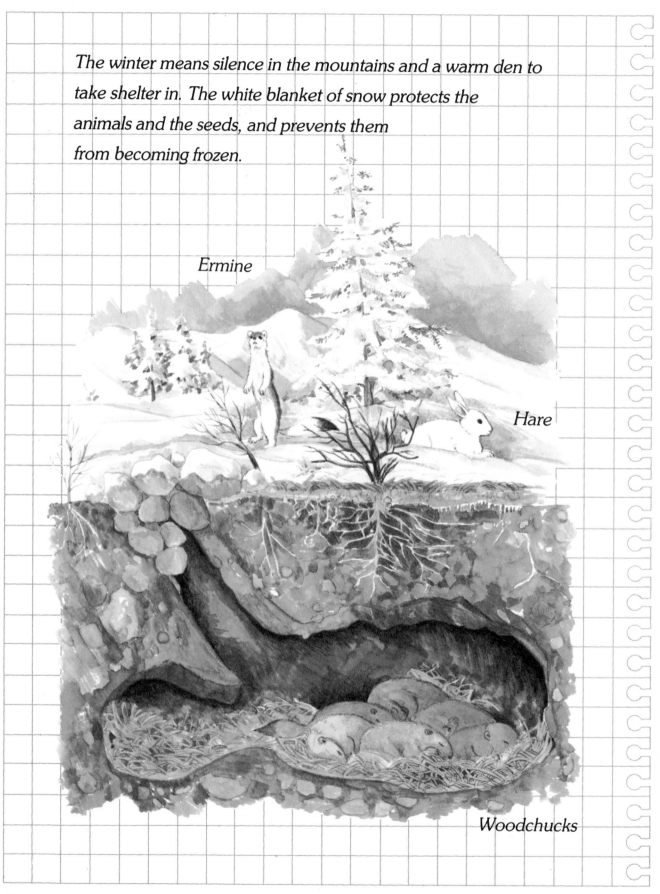

Ermine

Hare

Woodchucks

The goats keep warm by cuddling up in the stable, where they chew on the soft, sweet-smelling hay. Deep down in their burrow, the woodchucks are sleeping deeply, while the hare and the ermine blend with the snowy background in their white winter coats.

Goats

Winter means making do with little, with very little. The hind and her calf ease their hunger with some holly branches and some hard, dry tree bark. Luckily for them, their coats have become much thicker and provide them with good protection from the cold.

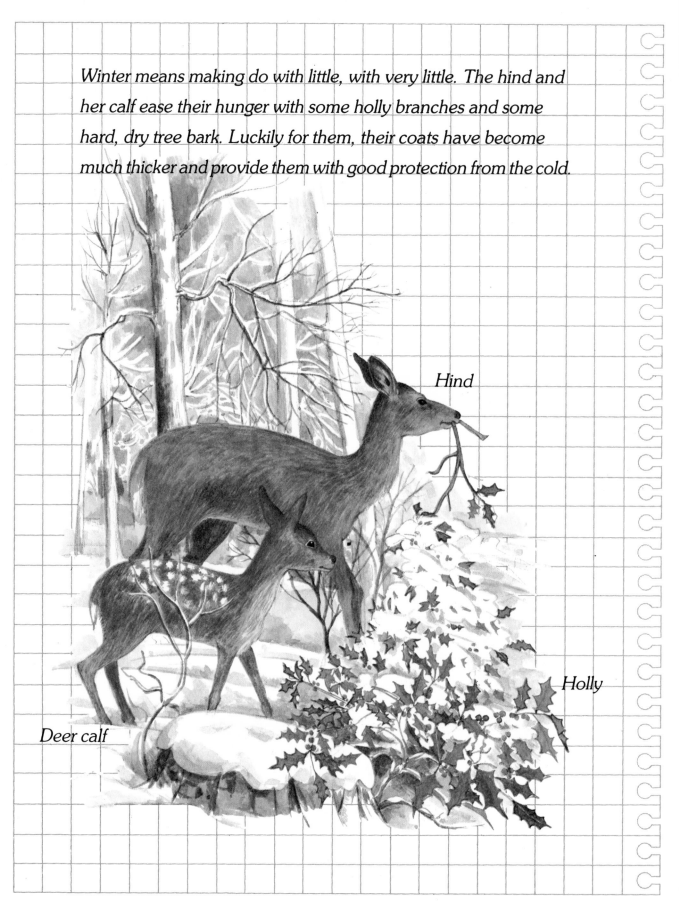

Hind

Holly

Deer calf

The birds search everywhere for the last of the berries, and peck up all the crumbs and the seeds that they can find. The squirrel has built up a good supply of nuts, as long as it can remember where it put them for safety!

Robin

Squirrel

Blackbird

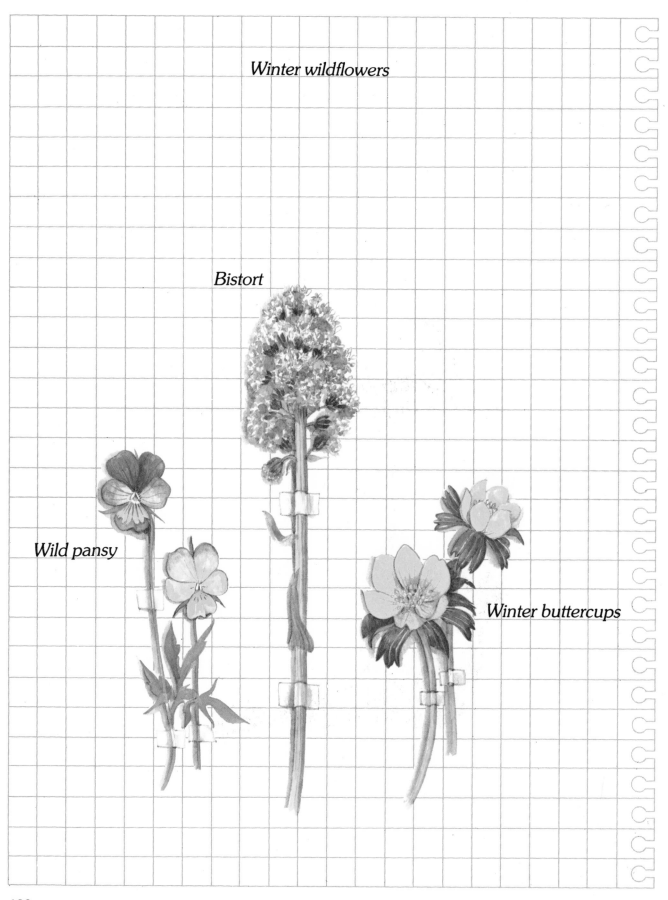

Winter wildflowers

Bistort

Wild pansy

Winter buttercups

The winter is also a time for wishing people happiness and abundance, beneath the symbol of the holly and the mistletoe woven together.

The holly reminds everyone of the joys of the Christmas festivities.

And the mistletoe brings good luck for the New Year.

Mistletoe

Holly

Contents